COOL
careers
for
girls

in
COMPUTERS

Also by the same authors

Cool Careers for Girls with Animals

Cool Careers for Girls in Sports

IMPACT PUBLICATIONS

COOL
careers
for
girls
in
COMPUTERS

Ceel Pasternak & Linda Thornburg

Liability/Warranty: The authors and publisher have made every attempt to provide the reader with accurate information. However, given constant changes in the
employment field, they make no claims that this information will remain accurate
at the time of reading. Furthermore, this information is presented for information
purposes only. The authors and publisher make no claims that using this information will guarantee the reader a job. The authors and publisher shall not be liable
for any loss or damages incurred in the process of following the advice presented in
this book.

Library of Congress Cataloging-in-Publication Data

Pasternak, Ceel, 1932-
    Cool careers for girls in computers / Ceel Pasternak & Linda Thornburg.
        p. cm.
    Includes bibliographical references and index. Summary: Profiles ten
women who work in the field of computers in such jobs as software engineer, network administrator, and systems analyst, and explains their duties and how they prepared for and got their positions.
    ISBN 1-57023-106-0 (hardcover)—ISBN 1-57023-103-6 (softcover)
    1. Computer science—Vocational guidance—Juvenile literature. 2. Women in
computer science—Juvenile literature [1. Women in computer science.
    2.Computer science—vocational guidance. 3. Occupations. 4. Vocational
guidance.] I. Thornburg, Linda,
    1949- . II. Title.
QA76.25.P37 1998
004'.023'73—dc21   98-48087
                                     CIP
                                      AC

Publisher: For information on Impact Publications, including current and forthcoming
publications, authors, press kits, bookstore, and submission requirements, visit Impact's
Web site: www.impactpublications.com

Publicity/Rights: For information on publicity, author interviews, and subsidiary rights,
contact the Public Relations and Marketing Department: Tel. 703/361-7300 or Fax
703/335-9486.

Sales/Distribution: All paperback bookstore sales are handled through Impact's trade dis-
tributor: National Book Network, 15200 NBN Way, Blue Ridge Summit, PA 17214, Tel. 1-
800-462-6420. All other sales and distribution inquiries should be directed to the
publisher: Sales Department, IMPACT PUBLICATIONS, 9104-N Manassas Dr., Manassas Park, VA 20111-5211, Tel. 703/361-7300, Fax 703/335-9486, or E-mail:
coolcareers@impactpublications.com

Contents

Careers in Computers

Why should you think about computers as a possible career choice? By studying the computer field, you can prepare yourself for work of amazing variety and depth. Computers touch just about every part of our modern lives. They are used to route telephone calls, to process bank records, to run cash registers, and to study weather. They are used in world-wide communications, in the manufacture of cars, in heating and cooling systems for your house, and in heart surgery. Computer work means far more than just sitting at a computer and inputting data. It can mean the power to access important research, to help the less fortunate, to forecast the future.

"Get a job in computers. You'll have unlimited opportunities." Everyone hears that advice, but what does it really mean to work with computers? To help you explore computer work, we've profiled 10 women in different computer jobs who love their work. You'll learn the duties and responsibilities that go with the job title, but you'll also learn about the women themselves —what drew them to the field of computers, how they found their first job, and how they took advantage of the opportunities presented to them.

These women continue to learn every day and to take on new responsibilities and challenges. Computer work is like that. Because the technology is changing so rapidly, you have to keep learning new things. All the women whose stories you'll read in this book love to solve problems and puzzles. All of them have good people skills. They know how to work on a team, and also how to be a leader. They are flexible and aware of how others think about things.

You'll read about women in jobs as

diverse as banking and real estate, women who run their own businesses, and women who are on the cutting edge of Internet communications. Some of them have been there almost since the beginning of the computer revolution. Others recently graduated from college. But one thing they all have in common is a love for the field and the desire to do new and exciting work.

We all want to do work we enjoy and to make a good living at it. Deciding on a career is a big step, usually made up of a lot of small decisions. Your career path will no doubt take many turns as you follow your talents, interests, and opportunities. Because your future includes more than work, you need to think about lifestyle choices, and how these will complement the type of work you do. So we've shown you how 10 women handle their personal lives, along with their work lives.

How To Use This Book

If you are wondering how to get a job in computers, this book is a good place to start. After you read each woman's story, you'll find a checklist with some clues about what type of person would be good in the particular job profiled. We've included some information about what salary you might expect to earn in jobs similar to those described. But remember that the jobs and job titles change fast, and the job you are reading about might not even be there when you get ready to go to work. Look for the sources for this information included here and check them periodically to find the latest information.

Getting Started Now

The last chapter, Getting Started on Your Own Career Path, suggests books to read, courses you should take in junior high and high school, and organizations that will help with more information. Many groups have both college student chapters and local chapters, which you may want to join to keep up with trends and changes in the computer field. Some groups have a mentor program. Finding someone who will take you under her or his wing and be there to answer questions you have about the field can help you decide what you should be doing now to prepare for a career in computers. These professional groups are also possible sources for scholarships. As you would expect, many of these groups have Internet addresses and can be contacted by email.

It's not too early to begin thinking about what work you would like to do as an adult. The earlier you identify the work you want, the earlier you can start preparing for a career. That includes taking the right courses in school now. And if you're interested in computers, don't be afraid to insist on your time with them at the library and at school, if you don't have a computer at home. Once you see how easy it is to use a computer, you won't want to stop working and playing on it.

We hope you enjoy the stories in this book. Look for our books on other careers as you begin thinking about what type of work might be right for you.

Basic Computer Glossary

Here are some of the computer terms you will find as we describe what each computer job is like.

codes, coding - a system of signals/commands used to give instruction to a computer, a piece of program text

computer science - the study of the principles and uses of computers

database - a large collection of data organized for rapid search and retrieval by the computer

database program - structures how information (records) is stored, how separate pieces of information (fields) relate to and affect one another, and how the overall system is organized. Those mentioned in this book include *D-Base, Oracle, Filemaker Pro, Cuadro*

DOS - (disk operating system) is one of the early operating systems; it requires the user to type in specific commands (see operating system)

encryption - creating codes and special symbols to represent specific meanings (*cryptography* is secret writing; the enciphering and deciphering of messages in secret code)

engineering - the application of science and mathematics by which the properties of matter and the sources of energy in nature are made useful to people; the design and manufacture of complex products (software engineering)

IBM - Herman Hollerith, inventor and statistician, in 1890 founded International Business Machines to develop new punch card technology. The firm grew to dominate the computer industry, especially mainframes for business, and is still active today

13

Internet - a communications network, originated by the federal government's Department of Defense and later used to connect universities, it allows the linking of computers worldwide for data interchange. Part of the network is called the World Wide Web

languages - a formal system of signs and symbols used to communicate with and program a computer; some languages are PASCAL, COBOL, BASIC, C++

mainframe - a large computer, its cabinet and internal circuits that can handle many tasks at the same time; the central processing unit (CPU) and primary memory of the computer

Macintosh - In the mid 1970s, Steve Wozniak and Steve Jobs started Apple Corporation to develop a user-friendly computer at a reasonable price; the Macintosh was the result. It was the first to give on-screen instruction in everyday language. Apple also introduced the mouse.

modem - a combined device that modulates and demodulates and converts signals produced by one type device (computer) to a form compatible with another (telephone)

network - a series of computers linked together for data exchange and data storage

NT - one of the newest operating systems by Microsoft

operating system - the interface between the user, the programs stored on the hardware, and the hardware itself

platform - a plan, design, or a support vehicle used for a particular activity or purpose, to carry a specific kind of equipment;

    hardware platform - a group of compatible computers that can run the same software;

    software platform - a major piece of software, (operating system or database) under which various smaller application programs can be designed to run

program - (noun) a sequence of coded instructions that can be inserted into a computer so it will operate a certain way; (verb) to work out a sequence of operations to be performed by a computer.

protocols - a set of rules/conventions governing the treatment and especially the formatting of data in an electronic communications system

simulation - a representation that functions in a similar way to a real function, (a computer simulation of the landing on Mars), sometimes called a computer model

server - the central processing unit and main memory that "serves" a network of computers

Silicon Valley - an area south of San Francisco, Calif., with lots of high-technology companies in the semiconductor industry that formed during the early 1970s, named for the silicon wafers used as semiconductor devices. New solid state technology allowed transistors, diodes and resistors to be carried on tiny silicon chips. This development led to smaller, less costly desktop computers or PCs.

UNIX - a computer operating system developed by Bell Labs when they were part of AT&T.

Windows - a computer operating system developed by Microsoft

World Wide Web, the Web - part of the Internet that is reached with an address http://www. plus the name of the Web site. Hyperlinks allow the users to jump from one Web address to another.

SOURCES OF SOME OF THE DEFINITIONS: *The Oxford Dictionary and Thesaurus.* (1996). NY: Oxford University Press; *Merriam Webster's Collegiate Dictionary.* (1995). 10th ed. Springfield, MA: Merriam-Webster, Inc.; *Random House Webster's College Dictionary* (1991). NY: Random House.

Robyn DeWees

SOFTWARE DEVELOPMENT MANAGER, **Earth Observing System Data and Operations System**, TRW Systems Integration Group.
TRW is a large company that has contracts with the federal government (especially the Defense Department) state and local governments, and commercial and international markets.

Major in Computer Engineering

Software Engineer

She Solves Problems Creatively

Robyn DeWees is in charge of hiring, leading, and managing a team of 40 software engineers who design and write the software that allows scientists to study what's happening in rain forests, oceans, deserts, and in the earth's atmosphere. Robyn is 33 years old. She loves her work and she's quite successful. But she says, if she could do it all over again, she'd be a football player. For fun, she plays middle line backer for The Kilroys, a coed football team in Arlington, VA. She and her husband, Jerrold, used to play softball, golf, and football together, but Robyn says they don't play as much together anymore because they are both too competitive.

Software Engineer

$28,000 to $40,000 with a B.S. degree

ROBYN'S CAREER PATH

Spends senior year at community college

Likes computers & sports at college

Creates databases for Navy

Inspired by her father

Robyn's father is a civil engineer, and he's very involved in helping people in his community. Robyn says she is very like him—more than either of her two brothers or her sister. "My father has been the biggest role model in my life," Robyn says. "I spend a lot of time trying to live within his light."

The youngest of four children, Robyn was sent to live with her mother's parents in Utica, NY, when her mother died. She was 12 days old. Every summer from the time she was 13 years old, she visited her father in Washington, DC.

As a girl, she was drawn to computers. At first, all she wanted to do was to take them apart to see how they worked. The only course in her high school was in computer programming, "so I thought I might try that," she says. "It led to a whole new side of computers for me. I absolutely loved my programming course. I enjoyed problem solving and working out the logic of writing programs." Robyn spent her senior year of high school at Mohawk Valley Community College in Utica, studying data processing.

civil engineer
an engineer who designs or maintains roads, bridges, dams, etc.

Studies plus
Sports

After high school, Robyn was accepted to The Catholic University of America in Washington, DC, just a few blocks from where her family lived, to study computer engineering. At that time it was a new study program combining electronics engineering and computer science. Her experience at the community college, while she was really still in high school, helped her, because the college subjects she chose to study at Catholic University were not easy. Computer engineering students had to understand both hardware (internal computer elements) and software

> ## "Go to job fairs. Explore what types of skills employers are looking for."

(source code). These people may design computers, cards, or chips. They may also write software like com-

puter scientists do and work with firmware, which is in-between hardware and software.

Although Robyn loved her studies, she wasn't the best student. She did well in hands-on laboratory work and could stay all day in the lab working

ity to work well with other students, which turned out to be just as important. Because software engineering is so difficult, students in Robyn's program studied together, and each helped the others get the difficult concepts that would allow them to

> "You may need a certain programming language to get your first job. Make sure you find out what that is and study it."

on problems, but she didn't like solving problems on paper. She did not take tests well, but she had the abil-

pass their courses and get the skills they needed to land jobs in the software industry.

Robyn has always loved sports. Throughout college she was visible on all sorts of varsity and intramural teams—volleyball, which she earned a letter in, softball, tennis, and flag football. A former Catholic University student, who had become a defense contractor in the area, recognized her from her sports activities when she registered with the school's Career Center. He offered her a part-time job, which turned into a full-time job before graduation.

'Everybody Makes Mistakes'

Robyn learns easily from the things that happen to her. One of her most valuable lessons came in her first job. Accidentally, she wiped out a lot of information on the computer of her company's customer—the United States Navy. Her boss and other executives in her company lectured her and were angered by the situation. At first Robyn was upset too, but she

defense contractor
A nongovernment organization that has a contract to do work for the U.S. military.

told herself that everybody makes mistakes, and the most important thing is to learn from them. That made her very calm, which impressed her boss. Everyone forgot the mistake within a month, but Robyn remembered it for years, because it taught her that making mistakes is the most valuable learning experience you can have—if you know how to profit from your mistakes.

Robyn got good experience on her first job, where she created databases and reports for the Navy so they could keep track of the parts they used to build ships. She learned how to listen to what customers wanted and to create systems that would make it easier for them to manipulate, store, and access information. At her second job, also for a defense contractor, Robyn worked on a system at the Pentagon that helped assign and schedule helicopters for Army, Navy, and Air Force officers. In working for defense contractors, Robyn learned to work with database programs like D-base and Oracle, how to use them to develop custom applications for customers, and how to work on many different computer platforms.

Later, Robyn learned how to manage projects. After a few years of working for small firms, she went job hunting at a technology job fair. She landed a job with the Harris Corporation, a big, multinational company with a new division developing information systems. She was assigned to a project for the Army. As part of a team of 10, she was responsible for building and maintaining the software that let the Army see how to get troops from one place to another.

manipulate information alter, edit, or move text or data on the computer

Pentagon the large five-sided building in the Washington D.C. area that houses the headquarters of the U.S. military forces.

Great Calculations at TRW

Robyn's next position was with TRW, which she joined in 1990. She worked on systems that let the Army see how best to get its materials from one place to the other. For example, if soldiers overseas in the Middle East needed boots, the system could give calculation that took 20 minutes to perform (searching the database) instead of the days that it had taken using the Army's old calculation. Robyn still gets compliments on having written the software that simplified the calculations used for

"You have to 'think outside of the box' and understand your customer."

the Army information about the places to take the boots from, how much time it would take to deliver them, and the closest places with the best supplies. It was here that Robyn created the piece of software she is most proud of. To find the location of needed materials, she created a logistics and shortened the time it took to get the information.

logistics the detailed organization and implementation of a plan or operation: the organization of moving, lodging and supplying troops and equipment.

"I looked at the problem differently than most people," Robyn says. "I broke it up into mini-calculations, so that you were doing five or six things at the same time. That probably improved the performance of the system about 100 percent. In order to get these kinds of results you have to 'think outside of the box' and understand your customer. I had to become a logistician for that time period."

Moving Up

Next, Robyn became the maintenance lead on her team. That meant she had to coordinate the testing of the software to make sure it worked. Robyn had an unusual way of testing the software. She first sat on the computer keyboard. "If I don't get an error message when I do that, then there is something wrong with your program," she told the software developers she was working with. She began to focus on testing methods, believing it was important to do testing systematically—to try to break the system before the customer did—so that all the bugs could be fixed before the software was used by the customer.

Soon, Robyn was promoted to technical leader for the team. Now she had even more responsibility. She had to help her team with their software development challenges by advising them when they needed it, keeping things on schedule, assigning work to team members, and helping team members evaluate their work to make sure they were doing a good job.

After a couple more promotions, Robyn moved to an exciting project called Mission to Planet Earth, a huge effort by NASA, TRW, and other companies to capture historical data about earth's weather and climate changes. Scientists will use this data, captured from satellites, to understand what sorts of changes are happening on earth. Robyn is the software development manager for the team that sends commands up to the satellite and receives the earth data. She makes sure the design for the software is right, defines the processes and procedures for the software developers she supervises, and makes sure all the problems are fixed.

"I could probably work 24 hours and not get it all done," Robyn says. "So I have to find ways to do things smarter and better." That includes delegating responsibility for some things to people on her team, concentrating on the things that she knows are most important, and communicating the mission and vision of the project to those on her team so everybody knows what they are supposed to be doing.

In her leisure time during the past few years, Robyn has been involved in a program to advise and counsel high school students who are interested in computer careers. She's also taught computer concepts to kids through a program called Junior Achievement. In 1997, she was named the director of a mentoring

program to give advice and counsel to women just entering the workforce, re-entering the workforce, or at a critical stage of their careers. Someday, Robyn says, she would like to merge her computer career with her career of public service, maybe helping kids to learn computers.

Carol Teasley

VICE PRESIDENT, **Systems Development, at Fannie Mae,** a corporation in Washington, DC, that makes sure money for home mortgages is available to home buyers.

Major in Mathematics, minor in English

Systems Analyst

Amazing What You Can Do With Mathematics

Carol enjoys her work because she loves mathematics, and she uses math to make computer systems work better. While doing her work, Carol talks with people in her company, analyzes how technology could help them do their jobs, and develops computer systems that make the jobs easier and the company more efficient. One of her department's projects is to prepare the company's computers for the year 2000, because now they can only recognize the years 1999 and lower.

Systems/Programmer Analyst

starting $25,200 to $30,000

average $32,000 to $52,000

SOURCE: *Career Information Center*

mortgage an agreement that says who owes money to whom for a piece of property; like a home or office building. If the money isn't paid back the person holding the mortgage gets the property.

CAROL'S CAREER PATH

Excels at
▼Stoney Brook school

Graduates
▼Bates College

Interns at
▼stock brokerage,
NYC

Growing up in
a Big family

Carol grew up on Long Island in New York in a small town called Setauket, where there were no sidewalks and no center line on the roads. Her family—mother, father, one sister, two older brothers, and one younger brother—did lots of things together. Maybe because her family was large "with high energy" and she had to stand up for herself, Carol listened to her own instincts and "did what felt right for her," she says. She played lots of team sports. She enjoyed playing in the woods and swimming, clamming, and water skiing at nearby beaches.

"My parents are my greatest in-

"Women are good at staying awake long hours."

flence and role models, and I admire them both," Carol says. "They expected a lot from us kids. My mother told me to 'have fun at college, and remember, B plus is not a bad grade.' My dad always said, 'Do it in your head,' so I learned to visualize and work things out in my head rather than on paper."

Joins Salomon
▼Bros. & travels

Marries John

Redesigns
▼systems at First
Boston, becomes
manager

Challenged
to Excel

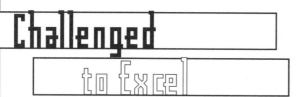

Carol did well in school. But when she came home after her sophomore year in high school with next year's schedule—jewelry shop, wood shop, French cooking, math, and two periods of gym—her mother was livid! So, at age 16, she was sent to a private school where she took German, history, English, math, and physics. At the new school, Stoney Brook, the principal told Carol, "Just because you did well in public school, you mustn't expect you'll repeat that here." That made her determined to prove him wrong, which she did. She graduated third in her class. She played basketball and field hockey, and she learned a lot about computers.

To help pay for private school, Carol got a job at a local restaurant. She went from working in the gift shop, to busing tables, to making crepes in the kitchen—a job that appealed to her love for precision and perfection. She worked at the restaurant during summers and every holiday break all through college.

crepes a French word meaning small, thin pancake

Carol knew she wanted to go to college, but she didn't have a particular career in mind. She wanted to explore all her options and have fun. "I went to Bates College in Maine. I took every kind of course, and finally, late in my junior year, I declared a math major and an English minor."

ers. She taught herself a couple of programming languages called BASIC and PASCAL.

"Cry all you want, but don't do it in front of anyone."

Carol loved being at a city college where she met many different groups of people. She volunteered for Big Sister activities. She did some tutoring and coaching and found she was good at it.

Bates was a Prime Computer beta site, in a Unix environment, and Carol spent a lot of time at those comput-

Big Sister The Big Brothers-Big Sisters Association matches boys and girls with men and women who volunteer to go places and spend time with them.

beta site places where people test software, finding out what is wrong so the company creating the software can fix its "bugs."

As a math major, Carol had to write a paper (an independent study and presentation). "There are two disciplines—**algebra**, which relies on the physical (tangible) and **calculus**, which relies on theory (conceptual). I prefer algebra, and I especially enjoy coding and encryption, so my paper was about that. I also used my math background for a paper in English. I analyzed the wonderful patterns and mathematical word play in Alice in Wonderland by Lewis Carroll, who was a mathematician."

Internship
Begins Career

Before she left college, Carol interviewed and got a job as a intern in corporate systems at Merrill Lynch, a brokerage firm in New York City. "There were 19 of us, about a third were women, and we were trained on their systems. It was my first time to work with the IBM operating system.

CAREER CHECKLIST ✓

This career is for you if you ...

- Love mathematics and solving puzzles

- Can take a challenge—if it "can't be done" you want to do it anyway

- Can work long hours and get along with little sleep

- Will stand up for yourself in all types of situations

brokerage a business of brokers, people who arrange the purchase and/or sale of securities, commodities, and real estate for others

GROUNDBREAKERS

After leaving Nova Scotia and a career as a music teacher, Mary Saunders (b.1848) used her manual dexterity to sell typewriters for a New York manufacturer.

But Saunders found the new machines' key layout cumbersome to use, so she redesigned it. Her revised keyboard became the standard for all typewriters and their computer descendants.

SOURCE: What Women Have Done calendar, Library of Congress.

I was assigned to work on the software that supported the branch offices throughout the country. During this time, we interns had to go to a class once a week and study their business—securities."

Carol met her future husband, John, at Merrill Lynch. He was one of the brokers. When they decided to date, Carol thought it would be best to leave Merrill Lynch. "It's not smart to date someone you have to work with. I had no trouble getting another job, because I had learned a lot, and employers wanted those skills."

"I was really lucky to get my next job at Salomon Brothers, an investment bank. I was hired because I had an ability they needed—I knew APL (the letters stand for A Programming Language). I had learned it in high

arbitrage quickly seizing an unusual and brief opportunity to buy or sell and make a profit—by selling and realizing a profit because the value went up higher than it should, OR by buying because the value went lower than it should and you know you can sell it at the regular higher value.

school as another way to do math. At this job I learned about arbitrage. I spent time on the trading floor on Wall Street, and my team and I had responsibility analyzing the arbitrage decision-support computer system. The computers were programmed to analyze what is happening in the market and notify traders when there is an anomaly—a glitch in prices that they know will correct itself. The traders must act at once to buy or sell."

"The trading floor is really a male bastion," says Carol. "I had to learn how to stand up for myself."

Then Carol was moved within Salomon Brothers to "probably the best job I've ever had. I traveled and the work was constantly changing. I never got bored, that's why I loved it," she says. Carol and five others traveled as a team to companies that Salomon was thinking of buying. Each of the six team members had a different expertise — Carol's was technology. The team members would analyze the company, then get together and discuss what they had

trading floor the main area of the New York Stock Exchange where trades—buying and selling—take place

Wall Street the name of a street in New York City's financial district where the New York Stock Exchange is located

anomaly the occurrence when a value which should not change, changes

bastion a fortified area, a stronghold, a protected place

learned, and recommend whether or not to buy the company. Carol learned to interview and "read" people—see through what people were saying to what was really going on. She learned to listen and see things from another's point of view. And she learned to defend and explain her own views.

But Salomon Brothers management began changing things, and Carol decided it was time to seek new challenges. She lined up a job at First Boston Corporation. But before starting that job, Carol married John, and they spent a two-week vacation in Mexico.

Carol's new job at First Boston was to redesign the computer systems that supported a lot of the administrative work in what the firm called the "back office." To do this she first had to learn how things worked. Carol enjoyed talking with people about their jobs, what they were doing and how it might be done differently. She analyzed how technology could help with the work and developed systems so that the computers would make the jobs easier and people more efficient.

At First Boston, Carol took her first management job, but she really

"Whom you work for is very important."

wanted to stay with the hands-on work she was doing. "In the systems field, between 6 and 10 years into your career, you really should have moved into management or people begin to doubt your abilities," says Carol. "Also, if I didn't take the job, they were going to give it to someone I felt I couldn't work for; so I became head of the area."

Planning a family

Shortly afterward at age 28, Carol had to be treated for skin cancer. She and her husband had planned on having children, but the doctor advised them to wait 5 years to be sure Carol was free of cancer. During these next years, Carol worked the long hours her job demanded—five or six days a week she'd work until 8 or 10p.m. She was steadily promoted and became a vice president. In his job at Merrill Lynch, John was also working long hours and doing a lot of traveling. When the 5 years passed, Carol knew she had to get a different job that didn't require such long hours, because she wanted to have a child.

She took a job at Standard & Poors. Because the company was small, Carol learned things she hadn't needed on other jobs—budgeting, how to hire and fire people, and labor laws. Carol worked here all through her pregnancy, had her son James-

Memorial Day weekend, and took 7 weeks maternity leave.

During those weeks, Carol and John decided they wanted to leave New York and that one parent would stay home with their son. John said he would be the at-home parent, and he retired from Merrill Lynch. Carol started job hunting.

The family moved to the Washington area when Carol hired on with Fannie Mae as a director. She put her leadership and people-management skills to good use, guiding the staff to high performance. She was quickly promoted. Carol is again working long hours (often 9 to 9), but she does take time for her family and an occasional vacation. Carol works out at a gym 2 or 3 times a week. She enjoys biking with the family, studies Spanish, and takes some time to counsel cancer patients. She plays golf to win and still loves to do puzzles.

Teresa Cason

ENGAGEMENT MANAGER, Sun Professional Services, at Sun Microsystems, a California based company whose people provide computer hardware, software (developers of JAVA), and consulting services to businesses throughout the world.

Major in Math and Statistics, minor in Psychology; MBA

Sales & Marketing
Executive

She Loves People, People Love Her

Teresa's job as a senior project manager and marketing executive is to bring in new business and consult with clients in her region. As one of the engagement managers, who service only key accounts, Teresa has the Sprint, MCI, and Bell Atlantic accounts. When she makes a sale, her company puts a team to work, usually in the customer's offices. Teresa keeps in touch with the team to see how things are going, and she keeps in touch with the customer to be sure everyone is satisfied. That part of her job is called client management—making sure that the client's business technology needs are taken care of by the Sun team.

Computer Sales and Marketing Professional

ranging from $115,200 to $200,000 plus bonuses and stock options

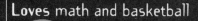

Teresa also finds new markets for her company's services. She learns how potential customers operate their businesses and their company's goals. Then she talks with her company's people to see if they can provide a product and service that will help that business meet its goals.

"Before I meet with a customer, I learn all I can about them." says Teresa. "I talk to my business contacts and I do research—get a financial profile from Dun & Bradstreet, read their annual report, and access EDGAR (the securities and exchange system) to get copies of companies' 10-K reports."

For example, Teresa might sell technology services like JAVA development or a relational database. Part of the team's work is to "migrate" the information in the old database to the new one. The team also has to reengineer how the user views the data and create new screens for viewing it. As companies put more of their business processes

Dun & Bradstreet - a Connecticut-based company founded in 1841 that provides credit reports on businesses; this information helps companies find out if a business pays its bills on time before selling to it

10-K Reports - If a company issues a registered security (stock, bond, commodity, etc.), it must file an annual report with the Security and Exchange Commission on form 10-K, reporting such items as total sales, revenue, pretax operating income, sales by product, management salaries and earnings, and its source and application of funds

Marketing and
proposal manager

Gets "techie" at Prime
Computer

Joins Oracle and
management

and information on computers, they have to have networks so employees can easily work with the data. Sun Microsystem runs solely on its networks, says Teresa. Her paycheck goes directly to the bank but she can view it on line, benefits information is on line, she fills out order forms on line, and she learned all about the company and its clients on line. Sun runs a real paperless office, says Teresa.

Teresa talks to a lot of people in her work. That's what she loves about her job. She learns about their com-

pany and tells them about her company. Often the people she meets know people at other businesses who might need the services of her company, and in this way she makes new contacts. She builds relationships with customers. She might take a customer to a baseball game or make deals over a game of golf. Teresa also meets people through groups like the Association for Women in Computing and Women in Technology, and she volunteers to make speeches at meetings and trade conferences.

Teresa believes one reason she is

JAVA - a programming language that moves easily to any hardware platform

relational database - allows data in a set of records to be accessed for use in another set of records, data "relate" to each other, data can be gathered from several sources and mixed into new records or reports

39

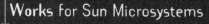

Gets MBA

Works for Sun Microsystems

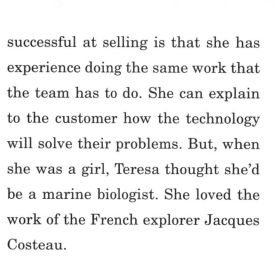

successful at selling is that she has experience doing the same work that the team has to do. She can explain to the customer how the technology will solve their problems. But, when she was a girl, Teresa thought she'd be a marine biologist. She loved the work of the French explorer Jacques Costeau.

Basketball
Taught Lesson

Teresa grew up in the small town of Verona, Virginia. Her parents still live in the same house. The youngest child (she has an older sister and brother), she liked to "visit" with her parents and other adults and listen to their stories. One of her favorite books was her father's old math textbook. The book was special because, when her parents were high school sweethearts, her mother had carved a heart on the cover of it.

Teresa was a tomboy, she says. Since there were few girls in her neighborhood, she mostly played softball and basketball with boys. When she started high school, she made the varsity team in girl's basketball. Playing basketball "taught me to be competitive, but also taught me to be a team player," says Teresa. "It taught me discipline, about winning and losing. As a team captain, I learned about leadership. I also learned there are people better than you. That may mean you're different and that's okay, or it may mean you've got to improve yourself."

Teresa took advanced courses in

geometry and calculus. "I had a wonderful math teacher," she says. "Even when I was struggling in college (Virginia Tech, Blacksburg, VA), she would meet with me and help me. I never thought something was wrong with me for asking for help—I'm not stupid, I'm ignorant, which is okay, because it meant I could learn."

In college, Teresa started out in computer science (she had given up on marine biology when she had to touch a fish), but didn't like learning how to write computer programs. She changed to a psychology major, but then changed to statistics and math, so she had to go to school for an extra summer session to make up for changing her mind.

Assertive
Job Hunt

Teresa's first job was in a grocery store, where she worked summers and school holidays during high school and college. "I enjoyed working with customers. I had a good time." Her first job in her career was in the Washington, DC area, where she moved after college to be near a certain young man, an important relationship at the time.

"My parents cosigned a loan so I had the money I needed to move," explains Teresa, "and I lived in a furnished apartment, paying rent month to month, no lease." To job hunt, Teresa went to a large office building, started at the top floor, and asked at each company if they had a job opening. She knew technical companies were interested in people with math and statistics skills. "I walked into a company called Integrated Systems Analyst and spoke to the person at the desk. I had no idea I was talking to the president. He asked me questions, took my resume, and later hired me."

The small company was doing business with the government, programming guided missiles, plus logistics, and other programs. Teresa used her math and physics to check the probability that the missile would hit its target. "Missiles are affected by gravity and thrust," says Teresa. "I had to prove air lift in college classes, so I understood what was needed. I love flying, I can tell by watching the wing exactly how a plane is lifting off."

Teresa got to know the marketing

grow. I was the first employee below executive level to get a bonus ($900). I worked there almost 3 years, but decided that while I loved marketing, I didn't like doing defense work. I got depressed thinking I was contributing to hurting people with those missiles."

"Technology keeps changing,
so don't be good at
just one thing,
it will keep you from other
opportunities."

person and volunteered to help him. "He taught me how to do marketing. I went on calls with him, he taught me how to do cost plus fixed-fee. He'd compare my pricing to his, that's how I learned. Eventually I did marketing for the company and helped it

Cost plus fixed-fee - a way of determining what to charge by taking the cost of an item or service and adding a previously decided charge that doesn't change (fixed fee).

Writing Proposals

Teresa's next job was for Harris Computer Systems, a large company that sells computer hardware to research companies. Here she did marketing as the proposal manager, responsible for all proposals to the federal government market. This job taught her a lot about putting in writing the details about the work Harris would do for the customer. She learned to create phrases so that details—like costs or hours of work—could be changed without canceling the agreement, thus losing the contract with the government agency.

"I liked the large company because it had the people, the policies, the resources, to be able to do what I told the customer we could do. The company had integrity and I could have integrity working for them. That is important to me. I was involved in pulling all the people together to make the contract happen. I was not

CAREER CHECKLIST ✓

This career is for you if you ...

- Are interested in meeting people and work well in a team

- Can listen well

- Like to match products with people who need them

- Think logically and analytically

- Are detail oriented

working on technical things then, but I taught myself Oracle, a relational database. I did it to manage my own work. Then we started using Oracle to keep competitive, to keep track of what other companies were doing."

Then, Teresa says. "I got 'swayed' away to Prime Computer, a large company that sells PCs and software. I wasn't looking to leave, but they contacted me. I had stayed in touch with some folks I met at a trade show and they told me about a marketing support analyst role that had opened up."

Improving
Technical Skills

Teresa had had no software engineering studies yet, but wanted to learn about computer operating systems, communications, and how to develop software. Here was an opportunity to improve her technical skills. After a 3-week "boot camp," where she met people from around the world, she took one class a quar-

ter, which the company paid for. Other studies she did on her own. She studied architecture in operating systems, then communications. She learned different protocols used to talk to computers. She learned to do backups and install software. She believed learning these technical skills would help her in marketing her company's products. "I feel I must learn and understand any new product so I can present it properly," says Teresa.

Her manager at Prime taught her about having a balance in her life between work and other things. Though she often worked long hours with no time for anything else, he'd make her take time off afterward for herself. Teresa worked on software support for the U.S. Senate (those of-

Marketing support analyst - a job that requires a person to analyze customer needs and how a company's products fit those needs.

fices that had selected Prime computers). When she was promoted to head technical person, she often traveled to the Massachusetts office, only getting home on weekends. She put the equipment through all kinds of tests and problems to find its weaknesses, then suggest how to improve it. "It is very important to the

Business Administration. She found it hard to find time for classes and studying because the job at Prime demanded more and more time. So she decided to leave and she took a job with the U.S. Department of Justice, which offered regular hours. Here she found the workplace was too rigid. She was used to a flexible

"Don't be afraid to say you don't know how, but add you'd love to do it."

company to know, because a customer would come in and say 'Can your machine do what you say?' and you'd show them the results of tests, and then they would make a multi-million dollar purchase."

Teresa next decided she wanted to go to graduate school to learn about business. She went to school at night, part time, and it took more than 5 years to earn her Master's in

workplace—come in late and work late, or work 14 hours one day to finish a project, take time off to run errands the next day. So, when she was contacted by the Oracle Corporation—a company that makes software, including the Oracle database—she accepted their job offer.

A Move Into Management

At Oracle, Teresa got experience managing projects. She moved from being a technician on a project, to doing some of the technical but also the being project leader, to being management. She put in long hours, but no travel, and she was able to continue her graduate studies. She was promoted, did marketing, still developed proposals, and learned how to manage her staff.

and integrate its various systems. (She had been talking with DMR people for six months before they persuaded her to take the job.) She sold DMR services and got new customers. She did a lot of guest speaking to let people know about this young company. One service she sold was the year 2000 work, and she was a member of the Information Technology Association of America Year 2000 Task Force. Many computers' inner clocks keep track of time and date, but only recognize years up to 1999. Changing them to recognize

"Don't be afraid to fail, just be afraid not to learn from the failure."

When Teresa left Oracle after 5 years, it was to open a Washington DC office for DMR Trecom, a company that helps businesses put up networks, get applications running,

the years 2000 and beyond before the year 2000 arrives is a big task. Some of her customers were banks and financial service firms.

While Teresa enjoyed this work,

🖥🖥🖥🖥🖥 HIGH TECH JOB OUTLOOK 🖥🖥🖥🖥🖥

Job Type	Jobs 1994–2005
computer systems analyst, engineers and scientists	from 84% to 101%
all other computer scientist	from 81% to 99%
operations research analysis	from 46% to 56%
engineering, mathematical and natural science managers	from 23% to 35%
statisticians and mathematical scientists	from 1% to 10%

Jobs that will shrink in numbers:

computer operator; electrical and electronic assemblers

SOURCE: *Handbook of U.S. Labor Statistics. (1997)*

success meant she was too senior to do what she really enjoyed. "I liked being a sales type person; I wanted to be managing a contract. I wanted to stay in middle management, interface with the customer."

Through her contacts Teresa found a job with Sun Microsystems. "I hope to use everything I've learned and keep learning," she says. "A major goal of mine is to some day own my own company, a small company."

When not working, Teresa is active in professional groups and in her church. She has a financial planner to help her with investments, she owns her own home, she works out every other day, and she just bought a second car—a 1998 Ford Explorer to make driving in snow easier. She keeps in touch with lots of people.

Elizabeth Gruben

PRESIDENT and CEO **of Telefusion Inc.**, a company that builds web sites and creates projects for customers in multimedia—animation film, video, computer modeling, and CD-ROM.

Law degree

Entrepreneur
Multimedia

Having Fun, Doing Good, Breaking New Ground

In a dimly lit room with large windows overlooking shrubs and trees, computer monitors show colorful cartoons, the inner ear, and a skeleton of a human hand. A video camera stands on a tripod and there is sound equipment and a separate soundproof room. This is the Telefusion laboratory where people work. It is a full-service multimedia and web development workroom that President and CEO Elizabeth Gruben designed.

Elizabeth started the company in June 1996 with a team of five people who had worked together to create a web site on the Internet for a large company called Telos Corporation. Now more than 30 people work for

Entrepreneur Compensation

People who start their own business may not earn any salary in the beginning. They invest their own money in the business, they get more money through loans or venture capital, and, until they make a profit or "go public" by selling stock, they probably pay themselves a small salary and put profits back into the business to help it grow. Sometimes when they sell the business, they sign a contract that pays them executive compensation to stay and manage the company.

Marries, has son, moves to San Jose

Does **paralegal** work, has son

Gets law degree, gets divorced

"A major quality in the people I hire is that they are open-minded and creative"

Telefusion. Most are women and men in their twenties, but some are still in high school and work part-time. About half are artists who can work well on a computer and are good in digital art and half are creative programmers. They have worked on a 5-minute show for a medical lecturer, a short animated cartoon advertising a web site, and demo disks.

One of the company's big projects was creating an interactive educa-tional web site—a virtual laboratory where high school students practiced doing blood tests. From "snapping on gloves because you're going to be handling blood" to writing up the results, students learned by "doing."

"This year we're creating a virtual neurobiology lab—dissecting a leech and isolating and determining cell

Silicon Valley
▼days at Telos

Marries,
▼moves to
DC area

Unix administrator
▼at NASA

types. It's all digital art and animation, and it's fun."

"We have a lot of fun," says Elizabeth. "A major quality in the people I hire is that they are open-minded and creative. We look for customers with four basics in mind. One, the work has to be interesting. Two, it has to be fun. Three, it has to do some good for the world, and finally, it has to have something about it that's never been done before. Even on days when it's a grind and the computer is not behaving, we still can't wait to get here because we find some fun in the work itself.

digital art - computer art or regular art converted to digits, by computer software.

An Eye for
Color

When Elizabeth was a girl, she missed out on a lot of fun because she was frequently sick. Born in Massachusetts, she moved with her parents to Los Angeles when she was 12. Her older brother and sister had already married. Gradually she became healthier. Then she started lifting weights and eventually became a "health nut."

"I always learned a lot, but didn't really get good grades in school," says Elizabeth. "I enjoyed creating things. I preferred molding clay pottery or casting jewelry to painting. I found I had a memory for color. I even thought about going into decorating."

51

One of Elizabeth's first jobs was color finishing in photo labs. In those days, color correction was a skill that took a "good eye," it wasn't done automatically by a machine. Elizabeth never planned her career path, but she was independent and earned her own money at a series of full- and part-time jobs. She used her talent for color and often sold her pottery and jewelry for extra money. She enjoyed her work.

"I always took care of myself. I didn't buy in to the idea my mother had, that you married 'a good provider' and he took care of you."

Her First Business
Home-Based

Elizabeth married and had a son. When the family moved to San Jose in 1977 so her husband could work there, she decided she wanted to make more money and have a real career. She went to word processing school where a fellow student told her about a job at an important law firm. She took a job there as a receptionist, hoping to move into their new word processing department.

Elizabeth began working with a paralegal—a professional who helps lawyers. Soon the law firm hired another receptionist, and Elizabeth did paralegal work full time. (In California paralegals can do anything a

"If you are really good at your job, they're never going to let you out of it. They figure they can never replace you. So what you do is find someone better and teach them everything you know, and then it's okay to promote you."

lawyer can do except take cases to court, but they have to work under a licensed attorney.) When her second son was born, Elizabeth took a year off to care for her son and earned money caring for another baby. Then, she decided to work out of her home as a freelance paralegal. She got more work than she could handle, so she contacted other paralegals she had met, and soon she was running her first business serving several clients.

freelance - a self-employed person who acts independently, offering her services to various organizations

GROUNDBREAKERS

Lady Augusta Ada Byron

(1815-1852),

Countess of Lovelace and

daughter of the poet Lord Byron,

working in the 1800s, is credited

as the world's first computer

programmer. She originated the

concept of using binary numbers,

a practice used in all modern

computers. In the 1970s, a

programming language adopted

by the U.S. Defense Department

was named ADA in her honor.

"It worked well for me. I worked out of my house, I was a real 'hippie,' hair down to my waist and younger son in a backpack when I went to gather information or deliver the work."

When she was 30, Elizabeth's friends talked her into getting a law degree. She went through a 4-year program at night because she needed to continue to earn money by working during the day. She passed the entry exam, and since she had not attended college, she also had to pass a lot of tests on basic college subjects and get a judge's permission to study the law, which she did.

"It was a very hard time. Each week I was studying 40 hours, going to classes 4 nights, working part-time, and spending any free time with my kids. It strained our marriage, and my husband and I parted, but on very friendly terms."

At the time of her divorce Elizabeth knew she would need a full-time job to support herself and her two children. Her husband was working at a computer consulting company called Telos Corporation. "I knew a lot of the people and liked them and the company," says Elizabeth. "They needed an account representative to sell their computer consulting services. My husband recommended me for the job, and I got it. So although I got my law degree at the end of the four years, I never worked as an attorney."

Silicon Valley
in the eighties

Elizabeth's new job was like a lawyer's in some ways. She carried a briefcase, had an office, and her customers were called clients. "But when I was doing the job right, everybody won. In law, even when you win, not everyone wins, usually something bad has happened. I realized the law wasn't creative or fun for me. I didn't like it. I had just allowed myself to be talked into it."

Elizabeth spent the next 15 years working for the Telos Corporation. "It was the 80s, it was Silicon Valley, the microprocessor had kicked in, Unix had kicked in, it was the boom years," she explains. Elizabeth became regional manager in just 3 years, still selling the company's services and going after contracts, but now also supervising other account managers. She learned how to hire people as the group grew from 20 to 90 employees. "Thirty of these talented people were women, and we were proud of that."

"It was a fun job." says Elizabeth, "because the people I had the opportunity to hire were amazingly interesting, fantastic, creative programmers. Many made more money than I did, and that was okay. We billed per hour, and our fee was a percentage. So the more hours people worked on the projects, the more the company made, and the better I looked to my management."

Elizabeth's role model was her supervisor, a woman about 7 years older who had hired her. "She was supportive. She encouraged me to ignore limitations; she helped bolster my self image. She saw that we got training—one year it was technical, the next year it was personal improvement. I learned about managing, creating job satisfaction for people, and how important it is to find and keep good people. We still keep in touch."

Elizabeth met her future husband, Roger, over the telephone. He worked for Telos at its New Jersey office. "All he had to do was say hello and that was it. I knew I was going to spend the rest of my life with him. I know it sounds ridiculous." When the couple married, they moved to the new Washington, DC area office of Telos Corp.

Getting Technical

Instead of selling contracted services, Elizabeth eventually began working technical jobs on Telos contracts. But she had a lot to learn. "I had to have help installing on my Mac, that's pretty bad." First, she was asked to recruit for an entry level-job as a Unix system administrator at NASA Goddard in Greenbelt, MD, working with the Mission Planet Earth project. When she asked the contract managers about the qualifications for the job, it was zero to 2 years. She said she had zero years, and they said great.

"As system administrator,' Elizabeth says, "I was responsible for keeping Unix up and running, backing up the data, making sure maintenance agreements were in place, programming the system for its regular tasks,

NASA Goddard - The U. S. National Aeronautics & Space Administration Goddard Space Flight Center, located at Greenbelt Md.

developing shell scrips in Unix. I had to learn 5 different versions of Unix in a very short time. It reminded me of law school—I was scared, in over my head, and I didn't think I was going to learn this stuff. But the customers knew what had to be done, they just didn't have time to do it, so they were very kind in teaching me. I read a lot, put in a lot of study time on my own. I also learned web development, which was in its early stages and became part of the job."

The NASA job was flexible and "part-time," mostly telecommuting. Elizabeth did it with a laptop, phone line, and a cell phone. She'd show up once or twice a week and fix things. But she could do almost everything from a remote location, in this case her home. "I worked 4 hours in the morning, took a break in the middle of the day, like gardening or something, then worked another 4 hours," she says. "My house was always clean. I traveled and visited friends because I could call in to work from anywhere in the country. I resurfaced my driveway—carried my cell phone

CAREER CHECKLIST ✓

This career is for you if you ...

Will take risks and can admit you don't know something but are willing to learn

Can lead people to do their best

Are open minded, not rigid in your thinking

Like doing lots of different things at one time

Think computers are great tools

Shell scripts - programs of commands that tell a computer to do certain tasks.

in my pocket and took off my work gloves to answer the trouble calls—it was great. But administration is very stressful, you're always dealing with people with problems."

Then, a former customer at Jet Propulsion Labs, called Elizabeth ally design a new language to do this." As the JPL project became more demanding, she left the NASA job.

"The new job required a lot of 'face time' with the customer. That was fun. I worked with some highly placed

"I traveled and visited friends because I could call in to work from anywhere in the country."

and asked if she knew someone who could to run a JPL project at the Pentagon to set up a web-based database. "That hadn't been done yet," says Elizabeth, "and there weren't the same tools there are today. It was to be part-time and flexible, so I did it. Actually, I managed the project, which was a Telos contract, I didn't actually do any of it. I found the people who could do it. They had to actu-

folks at the Pentagon, because we were putting on line the organizational chart for everyone at the Pentagon, which is still the world's largest office building—all of the armed forces are headquartered there."

Because of this web experience, Telos asked Elizabeth to become director of a new service area. She pulled together a team of five people to do the Telos web site, which was huge, so they got lots of experience. "When Telos started a new company, Interworks, they asked us all to go work for that company. We had done such good work that we were getting offers to do other web work. But when we'd go to our management with the offers, they'd say 'that's not the business we're in.' As it turned out," she says, "they didn't really need a team, they only needed one web person. So they decided to lay us off, but they did it gradually."

"I had already started working on a business plan, so when my friend Bill Pietsch and I were laid off, we started Telefusion as co-owners. As the other members of the team were laid off, they joined us. From the beginning we were being looked at by other companies wanting to buy a web-development business. After several months, SAIC Corporation bought us. So we're a small company that now belongs to a very large company."

Elizabeth understands the full technical capabilities of the Internet and the creative powers of her team.

This gives her a competitive edge in providing consulting to companies thinking of getting on the Web or doing a multimedia project.

Elizabeth works long hours in her start-up company. When she does take a break, she and her husband usually take a short vacation trip. Often they visit their granddaughter Monroe, child of Elizabeth's oldest son who is in the Air Force. Sometimes they ride on Roger's Harley motorcycle, a gift from Elizabeth, who enjoys riding as a passenger because "It's a lot of fun."

Geraldine MacDonald

VICE PRESIDENT, **AOLnet Operations, at America Online (AOL)**, a company that provides computer access to the Internet and other online services

Major in Psychology; Master's in Computer Science

Telecommunications and Online Services

AOL's Modem Lady

Gerry MacDonald loves being at the cutting edge of the telecommunications and entertainment industries. As the person responsible for adding more dial up telephone lines and modems for access to America Online within the United States, Gerry is always at the center of activity for AOL, which today has 10 million members throughout the world. Gerry's nickname is Modem Lady.

Gerry's job is to be sure there are enough telephone connections so AOL members throughout the United States can access the service through their computer modems. She and her staff contract with telecommunications companies and decide where and when to put in new telephone connections, making sure the

Senior Executive Compensation
Starts at $60,000 and goes up. *Executive compensation* is the total given to offset the heavy responsibilities that executives take on. In addition to salary, it can include bonuses, stock in the company, and other "perks" like club memberships, first class travel, a car—it varies with each organization. Senior executive compensation packages are approved by the stockholders.

connections can handle all the calls people want to make to connect with AOL. She has to know about the technology of network computing—how modems and network servers work and what the technical specifications for the telephone lines are. She has to plan ahead when to add more lines so people don't get busy signals because of heavy telephone traffic.

Gerry was recruited for her job at AOL because of her knowledge of network computing, an area she has worked in for many years. She was hired as AOL director of telecommunications and later promoted to vice president.

"It's great to be in this industry, which is so new," Gerry says. "There is no old boy network, so women have as much opportunity as men to do well. It doesn't matter what color or size you are, it just matters what you can do, how well you do the work."

Learns Basics at Binghamton

Gerry, her sister, and brother (both younger) grew up in New York City. She went to public school in the city and spent her free time ice skating in the winter, swimming and boating in the summer, and playing the guitar year around.

Gerry went to college at the State University of New York (SUNY) in Binghamton. She majored in experiential psychology, which meant lots of math and science classes. "I learned a lot about statistical analy-

Gets master's
degree, promoted
to Director

Daughter Erin born

Takes leave of
absence to work
near Silicon Valley

sis," she says, "and that turned out to be very important in working in computers in the early days."

After college she landed a job in an insurance company, where she had training to work with computers. The work consisted of programming a large, mainframe computer. This was in the late 1960s, when computers were very new. There was no such thing as a personal or desktop computer in those days, and there were very few courses you could take to learn about the big computers that existed. With her math and statistical analysis background, Gerry quickly picked up what she needed to learn.

Because she was so good at computer programming, she was offered at job at her university—SUNY Binghamton—working in the computer facility. Gerry spent 25 years working at Binghamton. She learned about new computer technology as it was invented, and worked to help members of both the business and other university communities understand and use network computing.

Gerry's first job at Binghamton was to do programming and to help Binghamton professors learn how to use the computer. The professors wanted to use the computer in their classrooms to show how scientific principles worked. For example, Gerry helped a professor create a simulation program so that students could test the effect of varying weights, fuel, and power on launching a rocket. This helped students understand the principles of physics.

After one year working at Binghamton, Gerry enrolled in the university's graduate program in computer science. By working full time and going to classes part time, Gerry was able to get her master's degree in computer science, which helped her to get management jobs in the computer field. "It's good that I did this while I was still fairly young. I had the time and the energy to study and work at the same time. The degree has helped me to get more and more senior positions in the computer field," she says. Because she worked for the university, she was able to get a lot of her tuition paid for.

Gerry's responsibilities then changed to include more teaching how to use the computer for both fac-

"Don't be afraid of the computer. Go to your local library or school computer laboratory and insist on your turn at the computer. You can't break it, so have fun with it."

ulty and students. She was promoted to director of academic computing at Binghamton. Now she was responsible for setting up short courses on how to use computers, for documenting computer programs that the computer facility staff created, and for setting up and managing a help desk for people who had questions about the computer.

"I liked the management responsibilities," she says. "It wasn't just myself I was responsible for then. I had to help set the priorities for the whole department and make sure we all met our goals."

Part-time
Interlude

In 1976 Gerry had a baby girl, Erin. Six years before, she had met and married her husband Bill, a professor of Geology at Binghamton. Gerry cut her work back to part time so she could spend more time with her daughter. She worked part time for a

CAREER CHECKLIST ✓

This career is for you if you ...

Want to be where the action is in computers

Love the idea of connecting people all over the world by computer

Are not afraid to present your views to different groups

Will work hard and study to get the education you need

65

few years, and then went back to full-time work.

"I'm glad I didn't just quit my job," Gerry says. "It would be very hard to get back into the workforce after 4 or 5 years of not working. This is especially true in the computer field, where things change so fast. But today, it's even easier for women to find ways to stay in the workforce after having a child. Young women don't need to choose between a career and motherhood these days. Companies have to accommodate the needs of working mothers much better than they had to in the past."

During this time, Gerry took a leave of absence from Binghamton and she and her husband went to Stanford University in Palo Alto, CA. There Gerry helped professors at Stanford learn how to use the computer. It was a time when California's Silicon Valley was growing by leaps and bounds, and Gerry found plenty of additional work consulting with people in industry about how computers could help in building business.

The Start of the Internet

Gerry continued to learn about computers and networking. Back at Binghamton she became involved in linking the school's computer to supercomputers at Cornell and the University of Pittsburgh. All across the country, schools were networking their computer facilities together in what was the beginning of the Internet.

Gerry became one of the founding members of a not-for-profit organization called NYSERnet (New York State Education and Research Network), which linked the computers at different schools in the region

leave of absence - a limited time away from work given to a person, often by a university or business, with the understanding that the person will return to the same job

together. She began to write papers for academic journals about computing and to speak at meetings where people from the computer community gathered to exchange ideas. She developed a national reputation as an expert in networking, and she served as the vice chairman of NYSERnet. Binghamton promoted her to associate vice president of computing for the entire campus, a position that required that she decide how to spend the school's money for computers and where they should go on campus.

In 1995, after 10 years of experience in networking computers together, Gerry was recruited for America Online. She moved to Reston, VA, where AOL is headquartered. "I'm totally addicted to the work," she says. "I can't imagine doing anything so exciting as this." But Gerry does find time to be with her family. Her husband is still working at Binghamton, so she commutes to New York to be with him. Her daughter is now in college, studying engineering.

not-for-profit organization - an organization whose business is conducted to serve its members or a cause but not to make a profit.

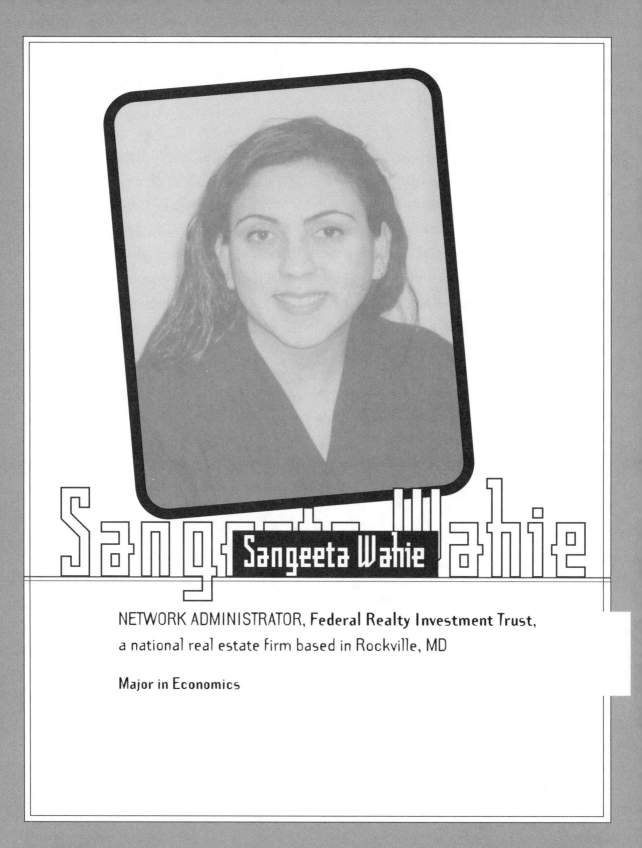

Sangeeta Wahie

NETWORK ADMINISTRATOR, **Federal Realty Investment Trust**,
a national real estate firm based in Rockville, MD

Major in Economics

Network
Administrator

from fear to fearlessness

At one time Sangeeta was afraid she would hurt the computer or destroy something if she tried to solve software problems or "opened the box." Now, her advice as she helps people at her company learn how new software works is, "Don't be afraid. If I can learn it, you can."

Helping people learn is just one of Sangeeta's duties as a network administrator. Sangeeta is responsible for all the service work related to the personal computers at her company. The computers are linked by a LAN, a local area network that connects all the PCs and printers and lets them all "talk" to each other. Some PCs have modems to dial out to the Internet and to send faxes. When there was no network, everyone had to put

Network Administrator

entry level $17,000
experienced, certified $27,000 to $37,000

SOURCE: *Encyclopedia of Career and Vocational Guidance. (1997). Chicago: J.G. Ferguson.*

SANGEETA'S CAREER PATH

Moves from
▼India
to U.S.

Plays football, loves
▼art, science

Studies abroad

data files on floppy disks and walk the disks over to another person who could put them in their disk drive and read them. Now everyone shares files by going to different directories on the LAN and reading the files on their own monitors.

cisions about which type of PC software to purchase to meet the company's needs. She selected network software that allowed her to control access to data.

Sangeeta also installs the software. She learns how it works and

"I finally realized it was okay to break it, there are people who will be able to fix it."

"I can set up who has access rights to directories of files," says Sangeeta. "For example, the president of the company may not want everyone to see his work. I can restrict access so only he and his secretary can get to those files." Sangeeta makes the de-

then teaches the staff. And she solves problems. She sits down at someone's desk and shows them how to create a table or how to do a calculation in a spreadsheet, or she talks to them over the phone and gives them help.

"Here we prefer that people save

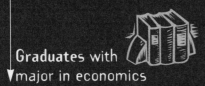
all their work to the network rather than to their PC." says Sangeeta. "We have allocated storage space for that on the network server. The big benefit is that we run a tape to back up all the day's work." Someone from

files.' We can find the files if that happens. We have cases every day when someone says they want to find a file they worked on months ago. We can find what they are looking for by checking through the old tapes. Soft-

"People will call me and say, 'I lost my files.' We can find the files if that happens."

a data storage firm picks up the tape each evening and returns it the next morning. Should some disaster, like a fire, happen at the office, the company can recover its business data; it isn't lost or destroyed.

"And we can help recover 'lost' files. People will call me and say, 'I lost my

ware files are easier to store and manage than paper copies stored in files and cabinets."

Sangeeta also does hands-on repair of the hardware. If someone is having trouble with their disk drive not taking the disk, the problem may be that the computer is damaged.

Sangeeta opens up the computer box and installs a new drive. And she installs new hardware, like adding a faster modem, and more memory.

Nine people work in the technology support department. Each, like Sangeeta, has a specialized area they are responsible for, like working on the older mainframe equipment or on database development. But they help each other when necessary.

Sangeeta keeps up with what's going on in the computer field, because she has to plan what technology the company may need in the coming year. She reads computer magazines and sometimes gets to go to a conference or a trade show to listen to experts. Mostly she is talking with other computer people, through electronic bulletin boards or the Internet. "A lot of my friends have been in the field and some are just entering the field. We have an informal forum to talk about what is happening."

Culture Shock

Sangeeta was born in New Delhi, India. Her parents moved to Maryland, near Washington, DC, when she was 5 years old. In the first grade, she learned that she was different from the other children. She spoke Hindi (pronounced hin dee), and she had a special class, separate from her classmates, to learn English. She went to a private Catholic school (although her religion is

Hindu) from 2nd through 7th grade. Every 2 years, the family returned to India in the summer for a month-long visit with relatives.

Sangeeta and one other girl played football with the boys at the school. "It was fun. I loved playing, but I slowly

When Sangeeta entered 9th grade, she was encouraged by her art teacher and often stayed after school to work on art projects. She wanted to be a painter, but she also played basketball (gave up football), was in an arts group, and was in an ex-

> "I loved playing football, but I slowly became aware of people's reaction—that I was not acting like a girl."

became aware of people's reaction—that I was not acting like a girl," says Sangeeta. "I think having a brother close to my age who encouraged me helped me keep up with sports, and I had him to defend me. Since they called me a tomboy, I made a point of dressing tomboy fashion."

change student group. In high school, she enjoyed English and advanced classes in science. She decided she wanted to be a biologist.

Deciding What to Study

Sangeeta went to the University of Maryland thinking she'd major in biology or zoology. But she missed her art—drawing and design—and decided that a career in architecture would be good for her. She had a lot of catching up to do, and friends helped her prepare a portfolio. But her application was turned down once. Discouraged, she did not try again.

But she had to select a major. She did well in math, but thought the only job available was teaching and she didn't want to do that. Her parents suggested she look into a business degree and later go for a MBA (master's in business administration). "I looked at the courses for economics and decided that would be my major," says Sangeeta, who had had advanced math, including calculus, in high school.

Sangeeta also played flag football at college. "There were more girls on the team," she says. "The team was part of the Indian students' association that I belonged to. We had cultural programs, social events, and softball and football teams."

One semester Sangeeta went to London, England, as part of a study-abroad program offered at her college. "I encourage everyone to do this. You get a different perspective being in a different country. You learn how they view other nationalities. Being Indian-American, I had the chance to see how they viewed Indians and Americans with different cultural, political and stereotypical outlooks."

portfolio - samples of an artist's work, also the large flat case used to carry drawings

Pushing Through
fear

When she graduated, after 5 and one-half years, Sangeeta wanted to start work right away to help pay back her parents. She planned to work a year, then start on her master's degree in economics. Her mother was working at the World Bank, and Sangeeta thought a job there would be good, especially because you could travel or work in other countries.

Sangeeta realized there would be few jobs she could get with her undergraduate economics degree. Since she was in a hurry to start working, she did a mass mailing applying for administrative jobs, general help, and office help. She took a clerk typist job at KPMG Peat-Marwick, a large management consulting firm.

"I was doing typing and filing, but I'd finish my work before the end of the day and have nothing to do. So, they asked me to help out the woman

World Bank - the International Bank for Reconstruction and Development, an organization administering economic aid among member nations

75

Occupation	No. of new jobs	% change from 1991
Computer engineers and scientists	236,00	112%
Systems Analysts	501,000	110%

SOURCE: *Career Information Center (6th ed.) Vol. 1, (1996) New York: MacMillan Library References USA*

who worked in the computer department. She was responsible for keeping the 200 Macintoshes up and running. I was doing clerical work for her and just beginning to learn a little about computers when she had to take a short-term disability leave. I was asked to do her job. I felt I could not possibly do it, but she said she'd help me over the phone."

During that time Sangeeta would cry at night, saying "I can't do this," but people depended on her and trusted her to solve problems. She'd decide "I'll go back to work tomorrow and see how it goes." Her supervisor, Vicki, taught her over the phone. She solved the problems, and gradually things got better. "When Vicki came

back, we worked together as a team. She is my role model. She was the Mac guru. After she left I became the Mac guru, and even became a source of help for other offices in our region."

Sangeeta stayed for 4 years. "It was so cool. I forgot all about getting an MBA; I got hooked on computers. I stayed late and came in early to take them apart and put them together, to play with the software. Teaching someone how to accomplish something on the computer really appeals to me."

Then Sangeeta noticed that the company was slowly replacing the Macs with IBM machines and she was concerned that her job fixing Macs would be phased out. She asked for training to learn about the IBM platform, DOS. When the company kept delaying, Sangeeta started some graduate-level night classes on her own, studying networks and PC components.

"My friends helped me a lot," says Sangeeta. "Several had computers at home, or they had a workshop and I went there, asked dumb questions, and experimented. I used computer-based tutorials too. I felt I couldn't hurt my friends' extra computer parts in the workshop. That's how I lost some of my fear."

Sangeeta also credits her last manager at KPMG with "pushing" her to succeed. "I can't possibly do this. You have the wrong person for the job," she would tell him at times. But he would insist she keep trying. "Just do it," he'd say. "I got more comfortable," says Sangeeta. "My biggest fear was that I'd scratch something, or unplug the wrong thing. I finally realized it was okay to break it, there are people who will be able to fix it."

As her knowledge increased, Sangeeta felt frustrated. She was the only person supporting 400 Mac users, but she wasn't learning anything new on the job. She decided to look for another job. After about a year of making contacts and going to interviews, she got a call about the "perfect" job. She found the company wanted someone familiar with network software to manage its network.

"Federal Realty is a great company, open to ideas and suggestions, and supportive of technology," says Sangeeta. "The computer group here has 9 staff supporting 200 people.

Sangeeta's support and teaching skills have helped her fiancee Sean. When they met through a friend 4 years ago, Sean had no need to know about computers. Then his job changed and he asked Sangeeta to teach him. "He was at the point where I was when I started learning," she says. "I'd help him over the phone or after work." Now they both have learned, when it comes to computers, "there's nothing to be afraid of." And Sean now knows some software programs that he has promised to teach Sangeeta.

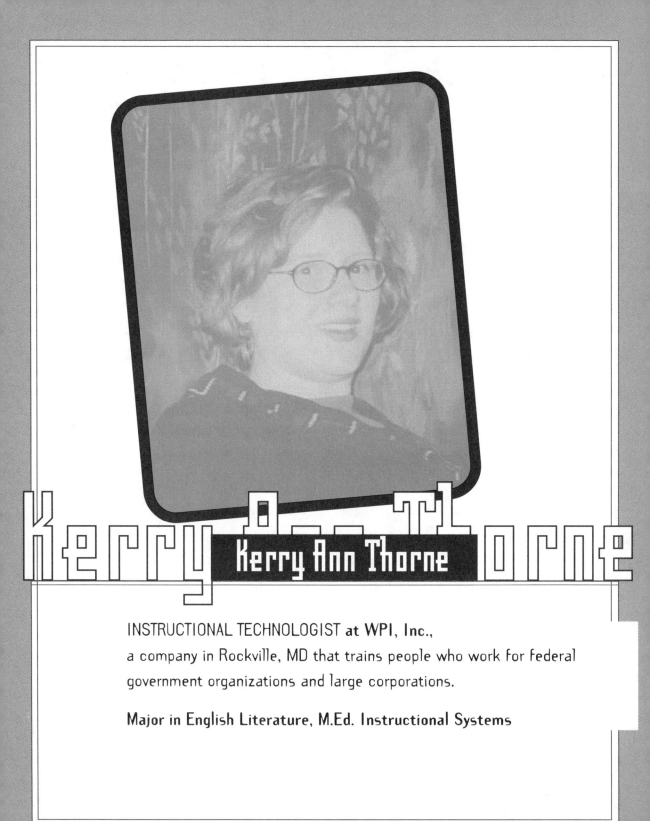

Kerry Ann Thorne

INSTRUCTIONAL TECHNOLOGIST at WPI, Inc.,
a company in Rockville, MD that trains people who work for federal
government organizations and large corporations.

Major in English Literature, M.Ed. Instructional Systems

Training and
Instructional
Technology

Teach Yourself, Help Provided

Kerry Ann Thorne is an instructional designer who helps to build Electronic Performance Support Systems (EPSS) and Web-based Training. EPSS are computer systems that help people who use computers in their work to do the work faster or better. They help people learn how to use difficult computer systems with just a little bit of instruction. Web-based training is teaching over the Internet's World Wide Web.

Kerry works in the performance support division of WPI, Inc. She loves working on a project that will make someone's life or job easier, and she likes working on a team with people who love computers. Generally her team includes one or more computer programmers, a software engi-

Instructional Technologist

average salary $35,000

neer, a graphic artist, and a project manager. An instructional designer has to know how to make learning easy. Kerry has to know how to make learning easy for people who use a computer, because they have a whole other job to do besides worrying how to make their computer work. Training has to occur with as little interruption to their regular job as possible.

As the instructional designer for EPSS, Kerry has to find out what people who frequently work on a computer need to learn to help them do their jobs better. Then she recommends ways to solve their problems using a computer help system. The help system allows the computer user to ask for help about a particular topic or problem and find the information that will help the user do what she wants to do.

To find out what type of a help system to build, Kerry spends time watching people do their jobs. Kerry likes to watch beginners work, because they make the most mistakes and ask the most questions. By watching them, Kerry can learn how to create a solution. She analyzes how they perform difficult tasks and then finds a way to make these tasks easier.

Kerry often travels to different places to see how people in one location may be using the computer differently than people who work for the same company or organization in another location. When one customer of Kerry's company wanted to streamline how it processed checks, Kerry

Goes to grad
▼ school, she and
dog live at farm

Gets assistantship with
▼ technology center

Internship with
▼ Recovery, Inc.

went and observed computer workers in Maryland, Virginia, Alabama, and Georgia. She watched workers to find out how fast they could work on the tasks they were given, what sorts of problems they had using the computer system, how they solved these problems, and what sort of help system would allow them to do their job faster. Some workers were good at finding shortcuts to repetitive tasks. For example, they found a way to program the computer so that it automatically would fill in fields when the information for the fields was the same. Part of what Kerry does is to capture these shortcuts and design them into the EPSS her team will build.

Kerry likes a lot of things about her job—the way she meets lots of people when she studies how they do their jobs, the flexibility she has to work either at the office or at home, and the fact that she travels to different places. Kerry often doesn't go into the office when she is working on a design; she stays home with her dog Eleanor Roosevelt and works at her dining room table. Kerry thinks working at home is the best because she can wear pajamas and no one cares.

Kerry's company sends her all over the United States, sometimes for a number of months. Kerry went to Seattle for 4 months, and the company provided her with an apartment

Eleanor Roosevelt -
(1884-1962) humanitarian and writer; wife of U.S. President Franklin Delano Roosevelt

and money for food for her and Eleanor Roosevelt (who got to go along). While she was there, she worked for the Boeing company, making online instruction for their workers. She got to tour Boeing's plane manufacturing plant and crawl inside unfinished planes to learn how they really were made so she could describe it in her instruction.

Long Distance
Learning

Kerry has a masters' degree in instructional design from Pennsylvania State University. When she began her master's program in 1994, the idea of delivering education over the Web was just beginning to be popular. She was the only person in her instructional design class who was really interested in delivering education long distances by computer. The rest of the class wanted to learn how to do instructional design for textbooks and classrooms or create classroom training for big companies.

Today this form of "distance" education and training is growing fast. Students are able to take many of their courses to earn a college degree or to gain the knowledge they need for their jobs by using the Web. A student can enroll in a course online, download the lessons, chat with the teacher and other students online, and even take the tests—all without leaving her house, if she has a computer.

Kerry became interested in this "distance learning" when she was working for the state of Pennsylvania. She had graduated from college with an English degree and had a hard time finding a job. Her mother suggested she try to find a job working for the state government, which was the biggest employer in her home town. She didn't like it. It was boring and it was hard and it didn't pay very much money. She knew she needed to think seriously about what type of work she wanted in her life and how to get the education she needed to get that type of work.

Kerry's friends, who also didn't like their jobs, took courses at night to try to get advanced degrees so they could find better jobs. Kerry admired them for that, but saw how tiring it was to work and go to school. Kerry thought it would have been great if her friends could have taken courses straight from home, using the computer. Kerry talked about her idea of online education with her parents and close friends. She was lucky. Her mom worked at the state's Department of Education and had many friends that knew a lot about education technology.

CAREER CHECKLIST ✓

This career is for you if you ...

- Can think of better ways to do things

- Like to make things that are useful

- Like to use technology to help people

- Are good at listening to people and asking questions.

- Like to travel

GROUNDBREAKERS

The U. S. Navy commissioned

the USS Hopper in 1997 in

honor of Navy Rear Admiral

Grace Murry Hopper,

pioneer of computerized data

automation in the naval service

and known for

COBOL language and

using the word bug for a

computer glitch.

This is the first destroyer and

only the second Navy ship

to be named after a woman.

A Job She Could
Love

Kerry interviewed lots of her mother's friends. She asked them what they liked about their jobs. She also interviewed friends of her mother who were in politics at the state level. Surprisingly, Kerry found the happiest people were people who hadn't always dreamt of what they were doing now, but loved their jobs and got really excited about their work. Kerry wanted to have a job she could love, too. She didn't want to be stuck in a dead-end job where she never had any challenges and life was basically boring.

Kerry wanted to find a way to go back to school full-time and study education technology. Finding a master's program in education technology meant she had to quit her existing job to move to a university. Finding a job that would support her at school would be hard. A lot of things seemed to stand in her way. How could she make a car payment when she was in school? Who would take care of her puppy? Kerry had decided to get a dog when she turned 21, against her parents' advice. Now she was worried about finding a place to live that would allow her to bring her dog. But she applied to college anyway, and decided she would worry after she had been accepted. And then she was accepted.

Kerry got an assistantship with a professor who ran the Jack Royer Center for Learning and Academic Technologies at Penn State, where she was studying. This was a real break. Kerry was able to get her tuition paid because of her assistantship. Fortunately, it is easy to find graduate assistantships in computer study. Everyone in Kerry's department that wanted an assistantship got one. She lived on a farm and worked as a nanny to pay for her room and board. And she was even able to bring her puppy, Eleanor Roo-

"Explore the Internet. You will find people who have similar interests. The great thing about the Internet is that no one knows how old you are. You can be the expert, no matter what your age."

sevelt, up to school to live with her on the farm.

As soon as Kerry finished her course work, she began looking for a job in the Washington, DC area. She was good at research by now. She knew how to use the Web to find all sorts of information, and she found out all about the Washington, DC area. She learned that it was a growing area for technology companies, and she knew she would be able to find work there. She found jobs advertised in newspapers by searching the Web, applied for three, went to Washington to interview, and was offered all three jobs. After a dissatisfy-ing stint with one company (where she didn't learn anything useful and felt like she was just a "warm body" because they were having trouble finding people that knew how to use a computer), she found her job at WPI, Inc., which she really loves.

Kerry loved the Internet from the moment she found out about it. She corresponded with a group of students in Wales while she was still in college, and she eventually got to fly to Wales to meet her email friends.

"Design your own Web page and put yourself out there. Share your interests with the world."

vertised in newspapers by searching the Web, applied for three, went to Washington to interview, and was offered all three jobs. After a dissatisfy-

She volunteered at a mental hospital while in college. When she got to graduate school she had to have an internship, and she decided she would create a Web page for a group that she met at the mental hospital. This group, called Recovery Inc., helps people cope with anxieties and problems by using common sense tactics. People using Recovery Inc. methods are encouraged to think about their problems in ways that help them to not be so frightened. They learn to do practical things that will alleviate their fears. Kerry designed a Web page for members of this group, and for visitors to the Web site. The fact that she designed this Web page helped her get her current job. And it also helped the people at Recovery, Inc.

Kerry is one of four sisters—the second oldest. The girls are all very different. The oldest, Kelly, has her own cleaning business and is a real entrepreneur. Karen, who comes next after Kerry, is a nurse and very compassionate. Kathleen, the youngest, is studying civil engineering. "I was always the intellectual one," Kerry says. "I always wanted to be known for my mind, because I wasn't good at sports, like my sisters."

Kerry's parents encouraged her to read and to aspire to be whatever she wanted to be. They expected her to go to graduate school. Her father, a stockbroker, was always taking courses as an adult and even taught once at a college. Her mother was acting Secretary of Education for the state of Pennsylvania at one time. History is one of Kerry's favorite subjects. She loves to read books about Great Britain's Winston Churchill and U.S. President Harry Truman, because they were people who paid attention to what they believed in, instead of being swayed by what other people were doing.

alleviate - to make more bearable, to relieve, lessen

stockbrokers - people who arrange the purchase and/or sale of securities like bonds and stocks for others

Lourdes Rodriguez

DATABASE ADMINISTRATOR for Garcia Consulting, McLean, Va.;
now on contract to Comptroller of the Currency, U.S. Treasury
Department, Washington, DC.

Major in Information Management and Technology, minor in Spanish

comptroller - a title for a financial officer.
Also "controller" a person in charge of expenditure

Database
Administrator

The Reign of the Database Queen

Lourdes Rodriguez is the "Database Queen," she says, and she loves it. "For the big things, no one can mess with the database except me." If the building has a power outage, Lourdes is responsible for shutting the system down. If one section runs out of space on a server, she is the one to increase the space. The database is Cuadra Star, which runs on a Unix platform, so she has to know the correct commands.

"This is not a stressful job," says Lourdes. "I work 8 to 4:30, Monday through Friday, and I don't take any 'baggage' home with me. It's great. I don't want to leave." But because Lourdes is part of a team hired at the Comptroller of the Currency on a 5-year contract, she will have to leave if

Database Administrator

college graduate $35,000 to $45,000

SOURCE: *Encyclopedia of Career and Vocational Guidance. (1997). Chicago: J.G. Ferguson.*

LOURDES' CAREER PATH

Skips 3rd grade

Studies, reads
5 books a week
or more

High school
honors course
in computers

her company, Garcia Consulting, isn't selected to do the work when this contract ends.

As database administrator, Lourdes does the daily tasks—running the datatape drive at the end of the day to back up the day's information, checking the tape every morning, running reports. The Comptroller of the Currency's databases (about 50) contain the corporate information about the national banking system and the more than 2,800 banks that the organization regulates as part of the U.S. Treasury Department. While the actual paper copies of the records are in files and on shelves, the database tells what the records are (every record has a bar code), where they are stored, and such things as the bank history, charter certificates, and applications for changes. For example,

banks have to file applications for permission to set up automatic teller machines or ATMs.

This information is available to the public under the Freedom of Information Act. The database helps people like reporters, lawyers, and bank customers locate information efficiently. Although she doesn't deal with the public, Lourdes helps the Comptroller, employees and the public by keeping the database current and running efficiently.

charter certificates - written grants of rights, description of an organization's functions, in this case describing functions of national banks

Freedom of Information Act - A law that gives individuals the right to request information gathered by the federal government

90

Works summers at
▼Express & dental
office

Graduates from
▼college

Moves to Maryland ,
▼develops database

Out of South Bronx
and the Projects

Lourdes was born and grew up in what she calls "a rough neighborhood, 20 blocks from Yankee Stadium, called Mott Haven. There were lots of drugs." It was New York City's South Bronx, where her parents settled after leaving Puerto Rico.

"I have good parents. They were strict. They put me in Catholic school where I skipped a grade; went from 2nd to 4th. Then I went to public high school and graduated at age 16."

Lourdes was a good student and she loved school. She had perfect attendance all 12 years. She did not like to stay after school for activities, so she'd come home, do her homework, then read. "I love to read. It is not unusual for me to read 5 or 6 books a week," she says. "The library was a block and a half from my house; I wore out my library card."

Some time during elementary school Lourdes got interested in computers. When she got to high school, she went into a concentrated honors course in computer technology. "I studied BASIC, COBOL, PASCAL, all those computer languages. But programming was tedious. I hated it," says Lourdes. "I knew I wanted to do something with computers, but I didn't know what. I 'sucked' in math and science. I took physics, did better in chemistry lab. In English I got straight A's. I did well in the computer classes. I liked tinkering, figuring things out, working with the software."

Meets Isaac via AOL

Database Administrator at Comptroller of Currency

Even though her parents hadn't gone to college, Lourdes knew she would go. She saw girls that she went to school with having children, and she didn't want to have kids when she

by all. "I wanted to go to the University of Southern California, but my folks said 'At age 16? I don't think so.' So I chose Syracuse University in upstate New York, where I was accepted

"Don't let life get you down. Keep an upbeat outlook on life and you'll be okay. If I could do it in the midst of guns, drugs, violence, you can do whatever you want."

was so young. Lourdes applied to eight or nine schools and got accepted

into the School of Information Studies, not the Computer Science School."

Lourdes loved college. She wouldn't change her 4 years there for anything. But during her time in college, her parents divorced and tuition increased from $18,000 a year to $22,000 a year. She got loans, she did work study, and relatives helped. "My mom was my rock through my college years," says Lourdes. During summer break and winter holidays Lourdes worked. The first summer she worked in retail at Express Ltd., and she still buys her clothes there. Then she found a job through a friend of her mother's as a receptionist in a dental office. "I loved working there. We had a lot of fun. The dentists were so nice to me."

Lourdes worked at the dental office after college while she was searching for a job. "I did my resumes on the computers at Kinko's, borrowed a typewriter to address the envelopes, then my mom mailed them. I went to my college placement office, and one of my former professors mentioned a job in Columbia, MD. I sent off a resume in June, then in August I got a call to come for an interview."

CAREER CHECKLIST ✓

This career is for you if you ...

- Have patience

- Have a positive outlook

- Are able to juggle different tasks

- Can deal well with "important people"

- Can be part of the office team

- Can handle a slow and a hectic pace

typewriter - a machine with keys for producing print-like characters one at a time on paper inserted around a roller

Lourdes had decided the summer of her junior year that she wanted to leave New York City. There was a shooting just outside her home. Minutes before on her way home she had walked past the man who got shot. "He was a drug lord or something," says Lourdes. "I said to myself, I have to get out of here."

Her college roommate lived in Maryland, so when Lourdes got the call to come for an interview she said yes. "My roommate's friend's husband met me at the bus station and took me to my roommate's house where I spent the night. The next day I dressed in

Developing a Database

Lourdes got the job, bought a used car with her family's help, and moved to Maryland, where she and her roommate shared an apartment. Her job was at Reference Point Foundation. Her title was program associate, but she was actually developing a new database. The nonprofit company was creating a database of information from catalogs (one was a medical catalog) for libraries. Lourdes was using

"I've learned so much from novels, I absorb the information."

my navy suit and they drove me to the interview. It went real well, but afterward I had to quickly change into my jeans in the restroom. They picked me up, and got me to the station for the 5 p.m. bus. The trip cost me $50."

software called Filemaker Pro. She enjoyed the work and the casual workplace, where she could wear jeans. But the company lost its funding and the people working on the project were let go.

Lourdes was eligible to collect unemployment checks while she looked for another job. "I kind of enjoyed myself. I wasn't stressed or depressed. I read lots of books." Finally she got an interview from answering a classified advertisement for the job she has now.

"The contract had just started, and at the interview I really hit it off with the boss. Then I had a second interview with the contract manager. I've been here more than 2 years and I love it. The dress is casual, but not jeans. I usually wear pants or, during summer, nice long dresses."

When she's not working, Lourdes is reading or planning her future with Isaac, her fiancé who is in computer sales. They met through America Online's romance connection 3 years ago. After many emails, Isaac helped her locate some software, so they exchanged phone numbers. Then they arranged a lunch date and have been together ever since.

Lisa King

COMPUTER SUPPORT SPECIALIST at the National Center on Education and the Economy, a nonprofit organization in Washington, DC, dedicated to creating new standards for education

Major in International Relations, minor in Journalism

nonprofit organization - an organization whose business is not conducted or maintained for the purpose of making a profit, but rather to serve a good cause

Computer Support Specialist

The Detective of Hardware Mysteries

The advantage in working for a small, nonprofit organization is that you get to do a lot of different things, and that's what appeals to Lisa King. She is the person who solves problems that employees might have with their personal computers and laptops, who installs new software, who teaches people how to use the software. She is the one who fixes things.

"The hardware is the part I really like, because it's like solving a mystery," says Lisa. "Something is not working and you have to trace where the power comes in, where it's coming out, and see where it's stopping. It's like being detective Columbo—if it's not this, and not this, then it must be that."

Computer Support Specialist

average $22,000 to $28,000

SOURCE: *Encyclopedia of Career and Vocational Guidance. (1997). Chicago: J.G. Ferguson.*

Lisa works with Macintosh computers except when she travels to Rochester, NY, where the accounting department has Windows NT. To diagnose and solve problems at the Center's locations outside Washington, Lisa uses a software program called Timbuktu. It allows Lisa to dial via modem into anyone's machine and control it. So if someone calls and says "My computer is acting funny," she dials in, uses her mouse and keyboard, and checks everything.

A lot of the people who work for Lisa's organization travel and have "duo-dock" laptops. That means that they can use the small, lightweight computers when they are out of the office. When they are in the office, they can just plug them into a docking station and get the big screen monitor and large keyboard. They don't have to fasten a lot of cables or download files.

The laptops are often in for repair. When users ask what was wrong, Lisa is careful to be diplomatic. "I can't say 'You broke it, or you dropped it.' A common problem is that the battery lead, the wire attaching the battery power to the computer, tends to get bent." It is Lisa's decision to either replace the logic board or unsolder the lead and put on a new one. "It's $275 for a logic board, but it only takes 10 cents worth of solder to put on a new lead, so the choice is easy."

What else does Lisa do? She recommends purchase of new equipment, configures it, installs memory and network cards in it, tests it, and ships it out or sets it up and trains staff. She replaces memory and modems. She reads magazines to keep up with what's new.

Growing up
With IBM

Born in Poughkeepsie, NY, Lisa is the daughter of an IBM pioneer. Her dad worked at IBM for 30 years, and he shared his tendency to tinker with radios and computers with his son and daughter. "If you were good, you could help. It was a treat," Lisa says. "I learned soldering when I was 8 years old, learned about transistors and capacitors. My brother got more interested in cars, but I enjoyed computers. It was like magic to me, what my dad could make the computer do." Lisa's dad had faith in her abilities. "My dad would say to me, when I brought my homework to him, 'Just think about it; you can figure it out.' He wouldn't just do it for me."

transistor - a semiconductor device with three connections capable of amplifying in addition to converting to direct current

capacitor - device of one or more pairs of conductors separated by insulators used to store an electric charge

Lisa's mother, who was a Girl Scout troop leader for a while, encouraged her to join Girl Scouts and a 4-H group. At 4-H she learned to speak to groups and demonstrate how to do something. In Girl Scouts she worked up to first class (equivalent to eagle scout) and in senior high was a leader of a junior troop. When she was in fourth grade, her grandmother came to live with the family. Every day after school she'd join her grandmother, who was watching the Watergate hearings on television. She got inspired to "go to Washington, DC, and help sweep away what was wrong."

Lisa praises her fourth and sixth grade teachers for giving her a love of learning and encouraging her to be ambitious—she wanted to work for the U. S. foreign service. Lisa also admires her great aunt, who is now 83. "She married at 14, raised her children, then taught school. But then rules changed and she had to get a degree to keep teaching. She got her GED, then went to college and graduated the same time as her son. She's an inspiration to me because she keeps learning."

In junior high school Lisa took Spanish and typing (it helped her earn money in college and made

using the keyboard quick and easy). She played clarinet in the high school marching band. She went to Guatemala as an exchange student; and the family hosted students from Mexico and El Salvador. That's when Lisa decided she loved to travel.

Lisa went to the University of Delaware in Newark, where she studied International Relations. "It was a well-rounded course and I learned so much. I did well in Spanish; but I wanted to find out if I was really good

Watergate hearings - in 1972, people connected with the Republican administration broke into the Democratic Party's national office, which was located in the Watergate building in Washington, DC. This burglary led to a national scandal. U.S. Congress held hearings that were broadcast over television, and then President Richard Nixon resigned.

at languages, so I took Arabic. I loved it. It's very phonetic and easy to read when you know the alphabet." Once a month the class would have a dinner, enjoy music, and talk with the native Arabs at the school.

Lisa worked different jobs at IBM during summers to help pay for school. One summer she worked in the electronics laboratory where her dad had worked. "I'd have to go get drawings for people to refer to and I'd see my dad's initials in the corner of the drawing."

Getting Hooked on Computers

When she graduated from college, Lisa took the difficult test given by the U.S. Foreign Service and did not pass. "I thought, well, maybe that's just not for me, working for the government. So I decided to get a job in Delaware. A lot of my college friends did the same. Then I got hooked on computers."

CAREER CHECKLIST ✓

This career is for you if you ...

Like to tinker with equipment

Have the patience to solve mysteries

Like to teach people

Need lots of new challenges

GROUNDBREAKERS

Bethel Carmichael, a research mathematician, is the first African American woman to go to sea on a military sealift command oceanographic research ship.

The project was to study properties of sound under water. She was responsible for the analysis of data on transmission loss and scattering strengths of sound.

SOURCE: Contributions of Black Women to America Vol II. (1982). Marianna W. Davis Ed.

Lisa was hired to do typing for the Delaware Emergency Planning Department, a state office located in an underground bombproof bunker. But she ended up doing a lot of work on computers. "They wanted to computerize the emergency operating plan, be able to call it up on screen, and work with it. Everything was new then; PCs were new. Nobody had more experience than anyone else, so if you could figure something out, you got to help."

Lisa stayed there over a year putting the plan on to the computers and installing the network. It was a small office and a fun time. Then people selling software to her company noticed Lisa and were impressed. They asked her to come to work for them in Maryland.

"Research Alternatives was close to Washington, DC, where I had always wanted to go, and the salary was good, so I took the job." But Lisa didn't realize how expensive it was to live in the Washington, DC area. She stayed a year, working on the software that created emergency management systems. The systems had maps to mark placement and movement of resources like fire trucks and

"You have to learn how to learn, because things keep changing."

emergency supplies. "The scanners were awful. We did hand digitizing, taking a pen pad and tracing things to get a better image to put into programs." She left because she needed to earn more money. She took an administrative job with the insurance company Mutual of Omaha.

futures and commodities brokers - people who arrange for the buying of goods and stock for future sales, and people who arrange for the buying and selling of commodities (articles or raw materials products like wheat)

Growing a
Great Job

Using an employment agency, Lisa got a job with the Futures Industry Association, whose members are futures and commodities brokers. "I started that job on Black Monday,

October 1987, the day the stock market dropped."

The organization had 3 computers and a database of 25 records when she started. "I was able to make the position what I wanted it to be. Since the members were using high-tech computers in their jobs, the board of directors were interested in moving ahead 'into the 90s,' and they were very supportive. I got the training and the resources I needed." When Lisa left after 7 years, all 15 employees had computers on their desks. The computers were networked, employees could send faxes from their computers, and the database had 15,000 records.

While working at Futures, Lisa earned good money and could afford her favorite pastime, traveling. She waited for bargain fares, then traveled to Paris, Australia, Russia, and other countries. She went with her roommate, or with a tour, or alone.

Lisa decided to leave Futures and look for something more challenging. She took some time to really think about her future. She had moved to Virginia and was in a serious relationship with a young man who owned his own company. She thought she'd like to run her own business. She became a manager at a Chesapeake Bagel shop. If she liked the work, she could buy a franchise Chesapeake Bagel shop of her own. "It was okay, but I found myself

"A well-rounded education is important."

franchise - an authorization granted to an individual by a company to sell its goods or service in a particular way (example, a fast-food store, a gas station)

spending more time tinkering with the computer functions than with running the business," says Lisa. "I realized that I needed to work with computers, not bagels."

Lisa worked as a secretarial temp while she looked for a computer job. She was a temp at the Center when she learned that the manager of information technology was planning on hiring a helper. She quickly gave him her resume, and she became the Center's computer support specialist. She is still learning and plans to learn about telecommunications next.

Lisa is now married to the young man she met through a local bulletin board chat group (he was the system operator, or sys op, and they chatted for 8 weeks before exchanging phone numbers). She and her husband hope to do a lot of traveling; their first trip together was to Paris.

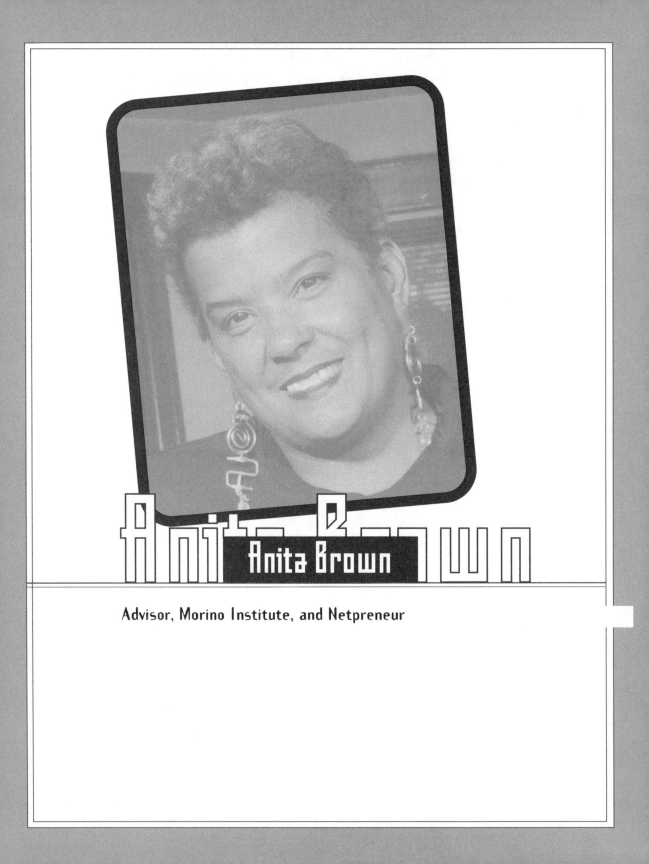

Anita Brown

Advisor, Morino Institute, and Netpreneur

Internet
Communicator

Miss D.C. Builds Virtual Communities

Anita Brown is a new type of entrepreneur—a netpreneur. The Morino Institute, which uses Anita's advice to bring more of the Washington, DC, African-American community into the netpreneur arena, defines a netpreneur as a creative risk taker, bridging entrepreneurship with the possibilities of the Internet. Netpreneurs create products and services that are for or are delivered over digital networks—from software to entertainment to information. They are developers and providers of hardware, tools, and infrastructure that help people use networks more effectively.

As an advisor to the Morino Institute, a nonprofit organization founded to encourage netpreneurs, Anita en-

Community Builder,
Email Queen

starting salary $24,000

nonprofit organization - an organization whose business is not conducted or maintained for the purpose of making a profit, but rather to serve a good cause

courages netpreneurship. She puts people in touch with others who have information they need; she shows people how to use the Internet to do electronic marketing and promotion of products and services; and she points people to places on the Internet where they can find the type of information they need.

Anita's speciality is network building. Not in the technical sense of putting together the connecting links for computers to talk to each other, but in the more people-oriented sense of bringing people with common goals and needs together by way of a computer network.

"If people don't go online by the year 2000 they will be left behind. It's important to get connected. You can find friends and contacts all over the world on the Internet."

Active in civil rights, black
▼empowerment

Works for consultant, plans
▼events

Discovers desktop
▼publishing; starts
own business

Personality
Plus

Anita is known as Miss D.C., a computer personality she developed that has allowed her to build, among other things, a virtual community called Black Geeks Online. Black Geeks is a 4,000-member organization that works to increase computer literacy and Internet access among African Americans. As Miss D.C., Anita manages several listservs with information for the community. And she manages the Black Geeks On-line website (*http://www.blackgeeks.net*). Black Geeks' main mission is to brainstorm ways to bring interactive technology to the African American community.

Anita also runs a "cybersalon" called Center Inn, where she encourages people to make the most of entrepreneurial and educational opportunities. She even conceived and produced an off-line event designed to bring Internet Technology (IT) to the "unconnected," called Taking IT to the Streets. It was billed as the coming out party for Black Geeks Online and was shown on local and national television. The comedian Sinbad was one of the sponsors.

Anita designed the help desk for NetNoir Online, the African American channel at America Online. She also wrote and edited stories and in-

listserv - an electronic mailing list where members share messages of common interest delivered by email.

109

formation that would appeal to new users of the Internet, America On-line, and NetNoir, and created a unique device to help people move around the site—a virtual concierge named SistahGeek.

Because she is now a well-known Internet personality, Anita has been invited to speak at meetings and events where entrepreneurs discuss the use of the Internet. She has also participated in many online forums where netpreneurism is discussed. She has been quoted in *Newsweek* magazine and *The Boston Globe* newspaper, as well as many other magazines and newspapers for business people.

Anita became interested in the Internet because she saw it as an opportunity to publicize tee shirts she designed as "wearable art." The tee

shirts have old sayings from the time when Anita and her friends were young in Washington, D.C., and other sayings from the past. The most popular is "Mama Said," which has sayings like "A hard heart makes a soft behind," and "You don't know what tired is." Anita has sold these tee shirts all over the United States by publicizing them over the Internet.

concierge - (in France a doorkeeper for apartment building) usually refers to a person in a hotel who speaks several languages and helps guests with advice and answers their questions, arranges tours of the area, and makes dinner reservations

Desktop Publishing
Talent

Anita began her entrepreneurial career after working a long time as a secretary, administrative assistant, and conference organizer. She discovered desktop publishing in the late 1980s and was impressed with the way she could do things using the computer that would take her hours and hours using a typewriter. Anita got more pleasure from her nonwork activities than from her paid job when she worked for someone else. She loved putting together newsletters for families and friends and helping people discover their own talents. "I realized one day that I'm a spiritual nurse in blue jeans," she says.

When she found the Macintosh and discovered desktop publishing, Anita managed to get an internship, where she could learn more about desktop publishing at the same time that she helped organizations create newsletters and other printed materials

CAREER CHECKLIST ✓

This career is for you if you ...

- Love people and can motivate them

- Are a risk taker

- Are creative and visual

- Are fascinated with new ideas and new trends

using the computer. She was 45 years old. "The idea of an internship at my age seemed strange to me, but there was no way that I wasn't going to learning how to use the computer, Anita was teaching herself about typography—what looks good in print. She was fascinated with how to size

"The day Dan Rather called
Washington, D.C. the murder
capital of the world,
I stopped watching television
news. Washington is full of
great people who do
creative things.
It's the gospel choir, the guy
who runs the restaurant
down the street.
It's people like you and me.

have more of that desktop publishing," Anita says.

At the same time that she was letters, what fonts you could choose to give words a different feeling when you saw them, and how to use the graphic arts to create meaning and message.

When she thought she knew enough, Anita quit her full-time job as an assistant and conference organizer and started her own business. She rented a Macintosh computer and a printer and began looking to her friends and acquaintances who needed desktop publishing services. She was fairly successful, but being an entrepreneur means you have to pay all the bills to run your company as well as to support yourself, and Anita needed more money. So she and some friends invented "The Bliss Kit," a package with everything a romantic couple needed for an evening together—candles, music, poetry, and good food. The Bliss Kit sold successfully and eventually led to the tee shirt business, which led to the Internet, and to the personality of Miss D.C.

Independent Spirit

Anita has learned a lot about herself since embarking on her career as a netpreneur. She knows that she learns differently than people used to say was the way you were supposed to learn. She learns by hearing and seeing things, not just by studying books. She likes the visual aspect of things and she likes the spoken word. She says this is why she didn't have a more traditional career, something some members of her family wanted for her. "My grandfather Ridgely taught anatomy at Howard University, and my family was prominent in Washington. But I couldn't be just a Ridgely girl. I got involved in the civil rights movement and black power movement during the late 60s and early 70s, and I really got into the idea of black empowerment. I discovered then that I had a talent for showing people how to find what they can do best."

A few years after the birth of her son, Shane, and her daughter, Vicki, Anita left her husband, because they weren't getting along very well. She returned to the house where she was raised to live with her mother and a woman who was like an aunt to her, although not related by blood. "It was hard being a child again, because you are always a child with your mamma," she says. She still lives in the same house and has her office there.

"To a large degree, netpreneurs are making the rules up as they go along," says Mario Morino, a software entrepreneur who sold his company for more than a billion dollars and then founded the Morino Institute. "What they say they need more than anything else is a community of their colleagues to share experiences, ideas, solutions and pitfalls."

Anita is helping to create that community. She knows that's what she does best.

Getting Started On Your
Own Career Path

Getting Started On Your Own Career Path

What to do now

To help you prepare for a career in computers, the women interviewed for this book recommend that you study the following in middle school, junior high, and high school:

Robyn DeWees

As much math and science as possible and any computer courses. Don't neglect written and verbal communication. A foreign language is helpful in today's global market.

Lourdes Rodriguez

If you want a good career, reading is fundamental. I've learned so much; there's a lot of history in romance novels and mysteries, and I keep learning.

Carol Teasley

College prep courses. Computer, math, science, also classes that rely on schematic drawing, like flowcharts. English and speech/communication.

Kerry Thorne

Psychology, computer applications, keyboarding.

Gerry MacDonald

Don't let anyone tell you that math and science classes aren't important for girls. If you want to work with computers, you will need as much math and science as possible to get into a good college program. But you also should take a foreign language, social studies, and English, because these are things you will need in college as well. Think about engineering as a college major. It's a great way to find a computer job after you've graduated from college. And make sure you find some work experience while you are in high school or college. If you want a good job in computers, you have to bring more than just your education to a company. You have to bring work experience.

Recommended reading

Carol Teasley

The Stock Market by Robin R. Young. (1991). Minneapolis: Lerner Publications.

Teresa Cason

What Color is Your Parachute by Richard Nelson Boles. Ten Speed Press.

Gerry McDonald

The Soul of the Machine by Tracy Kidder

Kerry Thorne

Cheaper By The Dozen by Frank B. Gilbreth and Ernestine Gilbreth. NY: Crowell.

Belles On Their Toes by Frank B. Gilbreth and Ernestine Gilbreth. (1984). Bantam Books.

Other

The Road Ahead by Bill Gates (revised). (1996). Penguin Books.

References:

Encyclopedia of Career and Vocational Guidance. (1997). Chicago: J. G. Ferguson

Peterson's Scholarships, Grants, and Prizes. (1997). Princeton, NJ: Peterson's.

www.petersons.com

Professional groups

Association for Women in Computing

Local chapters have scholarship and mentoring programs, reduced dues for student members, some college student chapters

41 Sutter Street, San Francisco, CA 94104

415 905-4663 (voice)

awc@awc-hq.org (email)

www.awc-hq.org

Association for Women in Science

Local chapters, mentoring program for college students, scholarships for those in Ph.D. programs.

1200 New York Ave., Suite 650; Washington, D.C. 20005

1-800-886-AWIS; 202 326-8940 (voice); 202 326-8960 (fax)

awis@awis.org (email)

www.awis.org

International Network of Women in Technology

The organization is dedicated to improving the status of women in technology and helping them advance to the highest levels of responsibility possible.

4641 Burnet Ave., Sherman Oaks, CA 91403

1-800-334-9484 (voice)

info@witi.com (email)

www.witi.com

The Society of Women Engineers

Local chapters and college student memberships. Administers approximately 90 scholarships annually that vary in amount from $200 to over $5000 per year. All SWE scholarships are open only to women majoring in engineering or computer science in a college or university with an ABET accredited program or in a SWE approved school.

120 Wall St., 11th Fl. New York, NY 10005-3920

(212) 509-9577 (voice) (212) 509-0224 (fax)

hq@swe.org (email)

www.swe.org

American Association for the Advancement of Science

A listing of career brochures, many targeted at women and minorities, is available by writing AAAS, Office of Opportunities in Science.

1200 New York Ave., Washington, DC 20005

(202) 826-6640 (voice)

www.aaas.org

IEEE Computer Society

Local and college student chapters; provides scholarships and publications. Can join just the Society or both the Society and the Institute of Electrical and Electronic Engineers.

1730 Massachusetts Ave., NW, Washington DC 20036

(202) 371-0101 (voice)

www.computer.org

Association of Information Technology Professionals (formerly Data Processing Management Association)

Provides professional education for members of IT profession. Student and local chapters.

315 South Northwest Highway, Ste 200; Park Ridge, IL 60068

(847) 825-8124 (voice)

www.aitp.org

Association for Computing Machinery

One of the oldest (1947)and largest educational and scientific groups. Offers many publications and conferences and has special interest groups. There are college student chapters, internships, contests, and employment assistance.

11 West 42nd St., 3rd Floor; New York NY 10036

(800) 342-6626 (voice)

http://info.acm.org

Getting started

The YWCA in several communities has job skills training for women. Check your local Y or contact WOW, which has a nation-wide network of organizations offering special training for women.

Wider Opportunities for Women

815 15th St. NW, Ste 916, Washington, DC 20005

(202) 638-3143 (voice)

www.w–o–w.org

Certification programs:

Networking Professional Association

Started in 1990 by certified NetWare engineers (CNE) trained by the Novell company. Sets standards for technical expertise and professionalism and has an independently run Certified Network Professional program.

401 North Michigan Ave., Chicago, IL 60611

(888) 379-0910, (312) 245-1043 (voice)

www.npa..org

Institute for the Certification of Computing Professionals

Runs a certification program. Provides study materials; generally tests are given at local Sylvan Technology Centers.

   2200 East Devon Ave., Ste 247, Des Plaines, IL 60018

   (847) 299-4280 (voice)

   http://www.iccp.org

Several computer companies have educational and certification programs. Among them are Novell, Microsoft, IBM, and UNIX. Contact the company's education department.

The Cisco Networking Academies Program

Cooperative venture between Cisco Systems Inc., a California-based network equipment company, and a few school districts. It is a 4-semester program for high school and college students on principles and practices of design, building, and maintaining networks capable of supporting national and global organizations.

   www.cisco.com/edu/academies

Also check with your local and state vocational and technical eduction and training programs.

A good place to start to discover the Internet

More than 700 sites listed here chosen by librarians to help young adults get acquainted with the Internet/World Wide Web. www.ala.org/parentspage/great-sites/

How COOL Are You?!

Cool girls like to DO things, not just sit around like couch potatoes. There are many things you can get involved in now to benefit your future. Some cool girls even know what careers they want (or think they want).

Not sure what you want to do? That's fine, too... the Cool Careers series can help you explore lots of careers with a number of great, easy to use tools! Learn where to go and to whom you should talk about different careers, as well as books to read and videos to see. Then, you're on the road to cool girl success!

Written especially for girls, this new series tells what it's like today for women in all types of jobs with special emphasis on nontraditional careers for women. The upbeat and informative pages provide answers to questions you want answered, such as:

- ✔ **What jobs do women find meaningful?**
- ✔ **What do women succeed at today?**
- ✔ **How did they prepare for these jobs?**
- ✔ **How did they find their job?**
- ✔ **What are their lives like?**
- ✔ **How do I find out more about this type of work?**

Each book profiles ten women who love their work. These women had dreams, but didn't always know what they wanted to be when they grew up. Zoologist Claudia Luke knew she wanted to work outdoors and that she was interested in animals, but she didn't even know what a zoologist was, much less what they did and how you got to be one. Elizabeth Gruben was going to be a lawyer until she discovered the world of Silicon Valley computers and started her own multimedia company. Mary Beth Quin grew up in Stowe, Vermont, where she skied competitively and taught skiing. Now she runs a ski school at a Virginia ski resort. These three women's stories appear with others in a new series of career books for young readers.

The Cool Careers for Girls series encourages career exploration and broadens girls' career horizons. It shows girls what it takes to succeed, by providing easy-to-read information about careers that young girls may not have considered because they didn't know about them. They learn from women who are in today's workplace—women who know what it takes today to get the job.

So GET WITH IT!
Start your
Cool Careers for Girls library
today...